DEVELOPING DEONTOLOGY

Ratio Book Series

Each book in the series is devoted to a philosophical topic of particular contemporary interest, and features invited contributions from leading authorities in the chosen field.

Volumes published so far:

DEVELOPING DEONTOLOGY: NEW ESSAYS IN ETHICAL THEORY

Edited by
BRAD HOOKER

WILEY-BLACKWELL

A John Wiley & Sons, Ltd., Publication

This edition first published 2012
Originally published as Volume 24, Issue 4 of *Ratio*
Chapters © 2012 The Authors
Book compilation © 2012 Blackwell Publishing Ltd

Blackwell Publishing was acquired by John Wiley & Sons in February 2007. Blackwell's publishing program has been merged with Wiley's global Scientific, Technical, and Medical business to form Wiley-Blackwell.

Registered Office
John Wiley & Sons Ltd, The Atrium, Southern Gate, Chichester, West Sussex, PO19 8SQ, United Kingdom

Editorial Offices
350 Main Street, Malden, MA 02148-5020, USA
9600 Garsington Road, Oxford, OX4 2DQ, UK
The Atrium, Southern Gate, Chichester, West Sussex, PO19 8SQ, UK

For details of our global editorial offices, for customer services, and for information about how to apply for permission to reuse the copyright material in this book please see our website at www.wiley.com/wiley-blackwell.

The right of Brad Hooker to be identified as the author of the editorial material in this work has been asserted in accordance with the UK Copyright, Designs and Patents Act 1988.

Wiley also publishes its books in a variety of electronic formats. Some content that appears in print may not be available in electronic books.

Designations used by companies to distinguish their products are often claimed as trademarks. All brand names and product names used in this book are trade names, service marks, trademarks or registered trademarks of their respective owners. The publisher is not associated with any product or vendor mentioned in this book. This publication is designed to provide accurate and authoritative information in regard to the subject matter covered. It is sold on the understanding that the publisher is not engaged in rendering professional services. If professional advice or other expert assistance is required, the services of a competent professional should be sought.

Library of Congress Cataloging-in-Publication Data

Developing deontology : new essays in ethical theory / edited by Brad Hooker.
    p. cm.
  Includes index.
  ISBN 978-1-4443-6194-0 (pbk.)
  1. Ethics. I. Hooker, Brad, 1957–
  BJ21.D48 2012
  171'.2–dc23

                                         2012001062

A catalogue record for this book is available from the British Library.

Set in 11 on 12 pt New Baskerville by Toppan Best-set Premedia Limited
Printed in Malaysia by Ho Printing (M) Sdn Bhd

1   2012

CONTENTS

NOTES ON CONTRIBUTORS

Elizabeth Harman is an associate professor of Philosophy and Human Values at Princeton University. Her articles include 'Creation Ethics: The Moral Status of Early Fetuses and the Ethics of Abortion' (*Philosophy and Public Affairs*) and ' "I'll Be Glad I Did It" Reasoning and the Significance of Future Desires' (*Philosophical Perspectives*).

David Owens became a professor at the University of Reading after having taught at University of Sheffield for 17 years. He has held visiting positions at London, Yale, Oxford's All Souls College, Sydney and Lublin. He is the author of *Causes and Coincidences* (Cambridge University Press, 1992), *Reason Without Freedom* (Routledge, 2002) and *Shaping the Normative Landscape* (Oxford University Press, 2012).

Michael Smith is McCosh Professor of Philosophy at Princeton University. He is the author of *The Moral Problem* (Blackwell, 1994) and *Ethics and the A Priori: Selected Essays on Moral Psychology and Meta-Ethics* (Cambridge University Press, 2004), and the co-author, with Frank Jackson and Philip Pettit, of *Mind, Morality, and Explanation: Selected Collaborations* (Oxford University Press, 2004).

Philip Stratton-Lake is a professor at the University of Reading. He is the author of *Kant, Duty, and Moral Worth* (Routledge, 2000) and the editor of *Ethical Intuitionism: Re-evaluations* (Oxford University Press, 2002), the new edition of W. D. Ross's *The Right and the Good* (Oxford University Press, 2002), and *On What We Owe to Each Other* (Blackwell, 2004).

Peter Vallentyne is Florence G. Kline Professor of Philosophy at the University of Missouri. He writes on issues of liberty and equality in the theory of justice (and left-libertarianism in particular) and, more recently, on enforcement rights (rights to protect primary rights). He is an associate editor of *Ethics*.

Ralph Wedgwood is a professor of Philosophy at the University of Southern California; he previously taught at Merton College, University of Oxford and at the Massachusetts Institute of Technology. He is the author of many articles on various aspects of ethics and epistemology, and of *The Nature of Normativity* (Oxford University Press, 2007).

DEONTOLOGICAL MORAL OBLIGATIONS AND NON-WELFARIST AGENT-RELATIVE VALUES

Michael Smith

Abstract
Many claim that a plausible moral theory would have to include a principle of beneficence, a principle telling us to produce goods that are both welfarist and agent-neutral. But when we think carefully about the necessary connection between moral obligations and reasons for action, we see that agents have two reasons for action, and two moral obligations: they must not interfere with any agent's exercise of his rational capacities and they must do what they can to make sure that agents have rational capacities to exercise. According to this distinctively deontological view of morality, though we are obliged to produce goods, the goods in question are non-welfarist and agent-relative. The value of welfare thus turns out to be, at best, instrumental.

Many theorists think that two related claims will occupy centre stage in any plausible moral theory. The first is that we should bring about more rather than less of what's of intrinsic value. The second is that welfare has intrinsic value. Putting these two claims together, they suppose that any plausible moral theory will tell us that we should produce more rather than less welfare.

Richard Arneson, who is typical of the theorists I have in mind, puts the point this way:

The concept of intrinsic value is not merely a building block in consequentialist theories, and if this concept (or the best revision of it we can construct) is found wanting, the loss would have wide reverberations. More is at stake than the status of consequentialism. I suspect any plausible nonconsequentialist morality would include as a component a principle of beneficence. In a consequentialist theory some beneficence principle is the sole fundamental principle; in a nonconsequentialist theory beneficence would be one principle among others. Whatever its exact contours, a beneficence principle to fill its role must rank some states of the world as better or worse, and direct us to bring about the better ones within the limits imposed by other principles that introduce moral constraints and moral options. We need some commensurability, a measurable notion of good. We need the idea of what is good simpliciter. (Arneson 2010, p. 741)

As Arneson's remarks make plain, the idea isn't just that we have obligations to bring about states of the world that track the amount of welfare in those states of the world. The idea is that we have obligations to bring about states of the world that track the amount of welfare in those states of the world *independently of whose welfare it is*. I take it that this is what Arneson is getting at with his talk of "intrinsic value" and "good simpiciter". The relevant contrast here is with the idea that our obligations track the amount of welfare we bring about, but that the welfare in question is (say) our own welfare, or the welfare of ourselves and our loved ones, or that of our community. To be more precise, then, Arneson thinks that any plausible moral theory will acknowledge that welfare has agent-neutral value, not merely agent-relative value, and that the agent-neutral value of welfare gives rise to an obligation to produce more rather than less welfare independently of whose welfare it is (Smith 2003).

Though I am sympathetic to the idea that any plausible moral theory will tell us that we should produce states of affairs with more rather than less value (Sen 1982; Sen 1988; Broome 1991; Dreier 1993; Smith 2003; Smith 2009), I think that the most plausible such theories will tell us that the values in question are *non-welfarist* and *agent-relative*. My disagreement with Arneson is therefore just about as complete as it could be. In what follows I want briefly to explain why I think that this is so. Though my reasons are somewhat abstract and require a significant detour in order to be spelled out, the substantive moral view which they lead me to embrace should sound familiar, as it is just a standard deontological view of the nature of our moral obligations, albeit one grounded in the existence of agent-relative values. Unfamiliar though my reasons might be, my hope is thus that they will suffice to show how and why a plausible moral theory might eschew both agent-neutral values and the obligations to which they would give rise.

1. A Familiar Puzzle

Whatever else it does, a moral theory will tell us what our moral obligations are. Since if we have a moral obligation to act in a certain way, it follows that we have a reason to act in that way, this entails that a moral theory will tell us what some of our reasons for action are (compare Darwall 1983, Darwall 2006). But since if we have a reason to act in a certain way, it follows that we would desire that we act in that way if we were to deliberate correctly, this entails that a moral theory will tell us which desires we would have if we were to deliberate correctly (compare Williams 1981 and Scanlon 1998 Appendix). This gives rise to a familiar puzzle.

Hume famously argues that there is a difference between the way in which reasons relate to beliefs, on the one hand, and desires, on the other (Hume 1740). Beliefs are states that purport to represent things as being the way they are. They are therefore "judgement-sensitive attitudes", to use Scanlon's term, because it follows that they are sensitive to the reasons that bear on the truth of the proposition believed (Scanlon 1998, ch. 1). Desires are, however, different. For while certain desires are sensitive to reasons that bear on the truth of propositions believed, these desires are all *extrinsic*. *Intrinsic* desires, by contrast, are not the sort of psychological state that could be sensitive to reasons. Hume thus holds that while extrinsic desires are judgement-sensitive attitudes, intrinsic desires are not.

By way of illustration, suppose I desire to have a pleasurable experience and believe that, since it would be pleasurable to eat a peach, the way for me to have a pleasurable experience is to eat a peach. Assuming that I am instrumentally rational, I will form an extrinsic desire to eat a peach, where this extrinsic desire is an amalgam of my desire to have a pleasurable experience and my belief about the effects of eating a peach on my pleasure: the extrinsic desire is just these two states hooked up in a state of readiness to cause my eating a peach if I don't want to do something else more (Smith 2004). Being an amalgam of desire and belief, my extrinsic desire is sensitive to reasons that bear upon the truth of the proposition that expresses the content of its belief component: that is, it is sensitive to reasons that bear on whether my eating a peach would be pleasurable. But the desire to have a pleasurable experience itself, assuming that it is not an amalgam of some further desire and belief – in other words, assuming that it is an intrinsic desire – is not sensitive to any reasons that bear upon the truth of anything. Though a sensitivity to reasons may change our extrinsic desires, it will do nothing to change our intrinsic desires, as no reasons have any impact on them. So, at any rate, Hume argues.

This is bad news, if it is true. For when we put this together with the claims about moral obligation and reasons for action described earlier, we derive a contradiction. Imagine a husband who has an obligation to treat his wife better than he does, but whose intrinsic desires are thoroughly nasty. Given that he has an obligation to treat his wife better than he does, it follows that he has a corresponding reason for action, and given that he has the corresponding reason for action, it follows that he would desire to treat his wife better than he does if he were to deliberate correctly. But given what Hume tells us about the relationship between reasons and intrinsic desires, it follows that his deliberating correctly would do nothing to change his intrinsic desires. No reasons to which he could be sensitive would have any impact on them. So long as the man we are imagining has made no deliberative error in deliberating *from* his intrinsic desires, it therefore follows that he would not desire to treat his wife better if he deliberated correctly. Contradiction.

2. Rethinking Hume's Strictures

To avoid this conclusion, we have to rethink Hume's strictures on the relationship between reasons and intrinsic desires. The assumption we have been making so far is that agents can deliberate correctly independently of the intrinsic desires that they happen to have. But, as I will now argue, it turns out that this assumption is false. In order to deliberate correctly, rational agents must have certain intrinsic desires (see also Smith 2010).

Imagine someone who believes for reasons by inferring that q from two premises: the premise that p and the premise that p implies q. Now imagine the moment at which he remembers having settled that p is the case, he is in the process of settling that p implies q, and he anticipates the possibility of going on to perform the inference and form the belief that q. What would an agent who has and exercises the capacity to believe that q for reasons have to be like at that very moment? Trivially, he would have to have and exercise the capacity to believe for reasons, as he is in the process of settling that p implies q. But are there any other psychological states that he would have to have or lack? It seems that there are. He would have to be able to rely on his past self who settled that p; he would have to be able to be vigilant at this very moment in settling that p implies q; and he would have to be able to rely on his future self to draw the inference that q. The mental attitudes constitutive of reliance and vigilance are thus both required.

Let's start by asking what would be required for our agent to be vigilant at this very moment. One way in which an agent may fail to believe for reasons, even when he has the capacity to believe for reasons, is by having an effective desire to believe something whether or not that thing is supported by reasons. This is what happens in wishful thinking. An agent who has and exercises the capacity to believe for reasons – our imagined agent who is in the process of settling that p implies q, for example – must therefore lack such an effective desire. Note, however, that there is more than one way in which he might lack such a desire. One would be to lack any desire at all to believe certain things rather than others, whether or not they are supported by reasons. But given that believing certain things rather than others, whether supported by reasons or not, is something that will contribute to the satisfaction of intrinsic desires that nearly everyone has, this is unrealistic. Even the ubiquitous desire to have pleasurable experiences tells in favour of acquiring certain beliefs, independently of whether they are supported by reasons. Think of the pleasure you derive from believing that your partner is faithful to you. If a fully rational agent is robustly to possess and fully exercise his capacity to believe for reasons, then he must have the wherewithal to cope with the potential deleterious effects of having ordinary desires like the desire to have pleasurable experiences.

Another, and much more realistic, way in which fully rational agents could be vigilant at this very moment, given that they may well have ordinary desires that augur in favour of their having certain beliefs rather than others, is thus by having a stronger desire not to allow those desires to be effective. Suppose, for example, that a fully rational agent desires to have pleasurable experiences, and suppose that this leads him to desire to believe that his partner is faithful to him, independently of the reasons. If he has a much stronger desire not to allow his exercise of his capacity to believe for reasons to be undermined, then the potentially deleterious effects of his desire to have pleasurable experiences would be mitigated. It would lead him to monitor himself to make sure that he isn't being led astray by that desire. Any agent, if he is robustly to possess and fully exercise the capacity to believe for reasons, must therefore have such a desire. Only so could he be on guard against the permanent possibility of engaging in wishful thinking.

Now let's focus on what's required for a fully rational agent to be able to rely on his past and future self. To be able to rely on his future self to draw the inference and believe that q, once he has settled that p implies q, an agent must similarly be on guard against the possibility of his presently having effective desires to undermine his future self's exercise of his capacity to believe for reasons. The way in which to do this, given the psychological resources available to him, is by having another desire like the one already posited, but with a slightly different content. For much the same reasons as before, then, an agent who robustly possesses and fully exercises the capacity to believe for reasons will have to desire that he does not undermine his own future exercises of his capacity to believe for reasons.

What if a fully rational agent foresees that he will be unable to play his role in the exercise of his capacity to believe for reasons in the future? Imagine, for example, that he is involved in a complex chain of reasoning and he foresees that, at some future stage, he will have a diminished capacity to believe for reasons. Perhaps he anticipates that he will have a debilitating headache, and he now has available a pill which, if taken later, would remove the headache. If he is robustly to possess and fully exercise his capacity to believe for reasons in such circumstances, then in order to be able to rely on his future self to play his part, it wouldn't be enough for him to desire not to undermine his future exercise of his capacity to believe for reasons. He would have to desire, more positively, that he now does what he can to help his future self have the required capacities so that he can play his part. In our example, the agent would have to desire to hold on to that pill so that his future self could take it. Absent such a desire, he could not rely on his future self to play his part.

Now consider an agent's past self. The agent we have been imagining, who robustly possesses and fully exercises the capacity to believe for reasons and is in the process of settling that p implies q, also has to be able to rely on his past self having settled that p for reasons, and not having had effective desires to interfere with his current exercise of his capacity to believe for reasons. This last is essential because only so will he be entitled to believe that he is not currently in the grip of an illusion, planted by his past self. In doing this, he seems to count not just on his past self's having possessed and exercised the capacity to believe for reasons, but also having had the very same standby desires as he currently has to ensure that he doesn't engage in wishful thinking or interference with his present or future self's exercise of his capacity. For so long as his past self had those same desires, his past self will indeed have exercised his capacity to believe for reasons and will not have interfered with his current self's exercise of his capacity to believe for reasons; he will not have planted an illusion.

Relatedly, if an agent is robustly to possess and fully exercise the capacity to believe for reasons, then he also has to be able to rely on the non-interference of other rational agents, assuming that there are such agents. He has to be entitled to believe that he isn't currently in the grip of illusion planted by them. It seems to me that in the special case in which the agent is a member of a community of fully rational agents, this too is grounded in the reasonableness of his supposing that all rational agents, if they are robustly to have and fully exercise their own capacities to believe for reasons, must desire not to interfere with other rational agents exercises of their capacities. For to suppose that rational agents do not extend their concern for non-interference to other rational agents in this way is to imagine that they make an arbitrary distinction between certain of those on whom they must rely – that they make a distinction between their reliance on themselves and their reliance on others – despite the fact that all of those on whom they must rely, insofar as they exercise their capacity to believe for reasons, have the very same interest in the non-interference of others as they have themselves. Since a rational agent would make no such arbitrary distinction, I take that it that his concern not to interfere extends to other rational agents as well.

A similar line of thought suggests that the more positive desire that we earlier saw a fully rational agent would have to have in order to rely on his future self, the positive desire to do what he can to help ensure that his future self has the capacity to believe for reasons, is also an instance of a more general desire that extends to rational agents as such. Fully rational agents must desire to do what they can to help rational agents as such have the required capacities to do their part in what's required for them to believe for reasons. Again, to suppose that rational agents do not extend the desire that they do what they can to ensure that they themselves have rational capacities in the future to other rational agents is to imagine that they make an arbitrary distinction between certain of those on whom they have to rely. To repeat, rational agents would make no such arbitrary distinction.

I said earlier that nothing in the argument turns on the initial focus on what's required to robustly exercise the capacity to believe for reasons. We could just as easily have made all of the same points by asking which desires an agent must possess if he is robustly to possess and fully exercise the capacity to be instrumentally rational: that is, if he is robustly to possess and fully exercise his capacity to form extrinsic desires in the light of his background intrinsic desires and his beliefs about what's required for their satisfaction. For in this case too, it seems that a fully rational agent could robustly possess and fully exercise his capacity only if he is on guard against the possibility of his own interference with his exercise of that very capacity. There is, however, an additional qualification in this case.

Given that an agent's background intrinsic desires might themselves lead him to interfere with his capacity to be instrumentally rational, or believe for reasons – think again about what the desire to have pleasurable experiences might lead an otherwise instrumentally rational agent to do – the required desires would have to be conditional in form. Fully rational agents would have to desire that they do not interfere with their exercise of their capacity to be instrumentally rational *on condition that*, by their exercising that very capacity, they do not form effective extrinsic desires to interfere with the exercise of their capacities to be instrumentally rational or believe for reasons. And note that this desire would also seem to be an instance of a more general desire that extends to all rational agents. Fully rational agents would have to desire that they do not interfere with any rational agent's exercise of their capacity to be instrumentally rational on condition that, by their exercising that capacity, those rational agents do not form effective extrinsic desires to interfere with the exercise of any other rational agent's, or their own, capacities to be instrumentally rational or believe for reasons (from here-on I will omit this qualification).

The desires described so far seem all to be instances of a pair of perfectly general desires whose content can be stated in the following terms: each fully rational agent desires not to interfere with any rational agent's exercise of his rational capacities, and they also desire that they do what they can to help agents have rational capacities to exercise. These desires, in turn, seem to be intrinsic, not extrinsic, because they don't depend on any belief that the things desired have some further feature that is desired. A fully rational agent simply has to desire these things themselves in order to function properly as a rational agent. The upshot is thus that, even though Hume was right that all reasons are truth-supporting considerations, he was wrong that it follows from this that no intrinsic desires are required by reason. Agents are required by reason to have certain intrinsic desires because, absent their possession, they could not robustly possess and fully exercise their rational capacities. In particular, could not robustly possess and fully exercise a sensitivity to truth-supporting considerations in the formation of their beliefs.

Given that correct deliberation is a matter of the possession and exercise of rational capacities, this in turn has a crucial bearing on what agents would desire if they were to deliberate correctly. What they would desire that they do if they were to deliberate correctly turns out to be fixed not by what they would desire, whatever intrinsic desires they might happen to have, but by what they would desire, whatever intrinsic desires they might happen to have, if they in addition had the two intrinsic desires that are required by reason. Correct deliberation is thus *deliberation from*, inter alia, this pair of intrinsic desires.

3. Moral Obligations, Reasons for Action, and Agent-relative Values

As I said at the very beginning, I am sympathetic to the idea that any plausible moral theory will tell us that we have a moral obligation to produce states of affairs with more rather than less value. However, as I see things, the most plausible such theories will tell us that the values in question are one and all *non-welfarist* and *agent-relative*. It should by now be clear why this is so, but in case it isn't, let me make it explicit.

Any moral theory, to be in the least plausible, will have to tell us why moral obligations entail reasons for action. Given that an agent has a reason for action just in case he would desire that he so acts if he were to deliberate correctly, and given Hume's strictures about the rational status of intrinsic desires, this gives rise to the puzzle addressed in the last section, the solution to which is to acknowledge, as against Hume, that any agent, if he is robustly to possess and fully exercise rational capacities, must have the pair of intrinsic desires described: he must desire not to interfere with any rational agent's exercise of his rational capacities, and he must also desire that he does what he can to help agents have rational capacities to exercise. In virtue of the fact that every agent's fully rational

counterpart has these desires, every agent has the same reasons for
action, and these reasons for action, I hereby conjecture, are
reasons to do what agents are morally obliged to do. Agents are
morally obliged not to interfere with any rational agent's exercise
of his rational capacities, and they are also morally obliged to do
what they can to make sure that agents have rational capacities to
exercise.

Consider again the husband who has an obligation to treat his
wife better than he does, but whose intrinsic desires are thoroughly
nasty. The nastiness of his intrinsic desires provides no challenge at
all to the idea that he has the two moral obligations just described.
For in order to deliberate correctly, the imagined husband would
have to robustly possess and fully exercise the capacities to believe
for reasons and be instrumentally rational, and in order to robustly
possess and fully exercise these capacities, he would have to intrinsically desire that he does not interfere with any rational agent's
exercise of his rational capacities, and he would have to intrinsically
desire to do what he can to make sure that agents have rational
capacities to exercise. But if the husband deliberates from these
desires – that is, if he forms extrinsic desires in the light of this pair
of intrinsic desires – then he would desire that he does not interfere
with his wife's exercise of her rational capacities, and he would also
desire to do what he can to make sure that his wife possesses
rational capacities. In other words, he would desire that he treats
her much better than he does. All that the nastiness of his intrinsic
desires would do is make him want to take steps to prevent them
from ever being effective.

Are the two moral obligations just described grounded in
values? It seems to me that they most certainly are. For according
to the dispositional theory of value that I have argued for in earlier
work, all that the desirability of some state of affairs, relative to
some agent, consists in is that state of affairs' being the object of
a desire that that agent would have if he were fully rational (Smith
1994). But since, as we have just seen, each fully rational agent
would desire two things – that he does not interfere with any
agent's exercise of his rational capacities and that he does what he
can to make sure that agents possesses rational capacities – and
given that each agent's desiring these two things is what explains
why he has corresponding reasons for action and moral obligations, it follows that his moral obligations are grounded in values.

Are these values agent-relative or agent-neutral? The values
in question are plainly agent-relative. They are agent-relative

because there is no way to characterize what is desirable without mentioning the agents themselves (Smith 2003). What each fully rational agent must desire, after all, is that *he himself* does not interfere with any rational agent's exercise of his capacities, not that every rational agent does so. And what each fully rational agent must also desire is that *he himself* does what he can to make sure that agents possesses rational capacities, not that every rational agent does what he can, and not that every agent possesses rational capacities whether or not anyone has to do anything at all to make sure that they possess them. What makes these states of affairs desirable, relative to each agent, is their being states of affairs in which the agent himself does not interfere with any rational agent's exercise of his capacities, or states of affairs in which the agent himself does what he can to make sure that agents possesses rational capacities. The values are thus agent-relative.

Are these agent-relative values welfarist or non-welfarist? The agent-relative values that ground the two moral obligations described above are plainly non-welfarist. For what turns out to be desirable is not pleasure as such, or the absence of pain, or anything else that constitutes an agent's welfare, but rather that an agent does what he can to make sure that agents possesses rational capacities, and that he does not interfere with any agent's exercise of his rational capacities. There will, of course, be a good deal of overlap between states of affairs in which (say) an agent does not interfere with any agent's exercise of his rational capacities, and those states of affairs in which there is an absence of pain, as causing pain is a very effective way to interfere with another agent's exercise of his rational capacities. Someone who has to focus all of his attention on dealing with pain typically lacks the psychic resources required to exercise his rational capacities. But the overlap is not perfect. If there are pains that have no effect on an agent's exercise of his rational capacities, then we have so far been given no reason to believe that these pains are undesirable, and if there are ways in which an agent's exercise of his rational capacities can be interfered with, but he suffers no loss of pleasure or welfare, then these acts of interference are undesirable even so. The values in question are thus plainly non-welfarist.

We are now in a position to see not just why it isn't true, but also why it is frankly implausible to suppose, that any plausible moral theory would include a principle of beneficence. A principle of beneficence purports to tell rational agents what they are morally obliged to do and hence what they have a reason to do. But given that an agent has a reason to act in a certain way only if he would desire that he acts in that way if he were to deliberate correctly, it follows that if any plausible moral theory had to include a principle of beneficence, grounded in the agent-neutral value of welfare, then any agent who robustly possesses and fully exercises his capacity to believe for reasons and be instrumentally rational would have to desire that the world contains more welfare rather than less. But what is the connection supposed to be between such a free-floating concern for welfare and the robust possession and full exercise of rational capacities? The answer is that there is no connection at all. The ideas are orthogonal to each other. The same cannot be said, however, of the desires not to interfere with any agent's exercise of his rational capacities and to make sure that agents have rational capacities to exercise. As I have tried to argue, the connection between these desires and an agent's robust possession and full exercise of rational capacities is, more or less, transparent.

4. Conclusion

According to the abstract line of argument developed here, agents have two moral obligations. They are morally obliged not to interfere with any agent's exercise of his rational capacities and they are also morally obliged to do what they can to make sure that agents have rational capacities to exercise. Though these claims doubtless require much more in the way of defence than I have given them here, I hope I have said enough to make them sound at least plausible. If so, then it will have to be agreed that at least one plausible moral theory, the theory according to which agents have the two moral obligations just described, need not include a principle of beneficence, and, more generally, that such a theory could eschew both agent-neutral values and the moral obligations to which they would give rise. For though this theory does ground moral obligations in values, the values in question are all agent-relative and non-welfarist.

References

Arneson, Richard J. (2010). 'Good, Period', *Analysis* (70) pp. 731–44.
Broome, John (1991). *Weighing Goods* (Oxford: Blackwell).
Darwall, Stephen (1983). *Impartial Reason* (Ithaca: Cornell University Press).

—— (2006). *The Second-Person Standpoint: Morality, Respect, and Accountability* (Cambridge: Harvard University Press).

Dreier, James (1993). 'Structures of Normative Theories', *The Monist* (76) pp. 22–40.

Hume, David (1740). *A Treatise of Human Nature* (Oxford: Clarendon Press, 1740/1968).

Scanlon, Thomas M. (1998). *What We Owe To Each Other* (Cambridge: Harvard University Press).

Sen, Amartya (1982). 'Rights and Agency', *Philosophy and Public Affairs* (11) pp. 3–39.

—— (1988). 'Evaluator Relativity and Consequential Evaluation', in *Philosophy and Public Affairs* (12) pp. 113–132.

Smith, Michael (1994). *The Moral Problem* (Oxford: Blackwell Publishers).

—— (2003). 'Neutral and Relative Value after Moore', *Ethics,* Centenary Symposium on G.E.Moore's *Principia Ethica* (113) pp. 576–98.

—— (2004). 'Instrumental Desires, Instrumental Rationality', *Proceedings of the Aristotelian Society Supplementary Volume* (78) pp. 93–109.

—— (2009). 'Two Kinds of Consequentialism', *Philosophical Issues* (19), pp. 257–72.

—— (2010). 'Beyond the Error Theory', in *A World Without Values: Essays on John Mackie's Moral Error Theory* edited by Richard Joyce and Simon Kirchin (New York: Springer) pp. 119–39.

Williams, Bernard (1981). 'Internal and External Reasons', reprinted in his *Moral Luck* (Cambridge: Cambridge University Press).

2

RECALCITRANT PLURALISM

Philip Stratton-Lake

Abstract

In this paper I argue that the best form of deontology is one understood in terms of prima facie duties. I outline how these duties are to be understood and show how they offer a plausible and elegant connection between the reason why we ought to do certain acts, the normative reasons we have to do these acts, the reason why moral agents will do them, and the reasons certain people have to resent someone who does not do them. I then argue that this form of deontology makes it harder to unify a pluralistic ethics under a single consequentialist principle in a plausible way, and illustrate this with reference to Rob Shaver's consequentialist arguments.

Introduction: Moral foundationalism

The various forms of deontology and consequentialism are foundationalist theories. They are foundationalist in the sense that they both offer differing views about what the most fundamental moral principles are, and maintain that all of our obligations can be derived from these principles. Principles are *moral* in the relevant sense here in so far as they specify what our prima facie, or actual duties or obligations are.

Although one might make quite valid distinctions between thin deontic notions such as right, duty, obligation, ought, required, etc, in this paper I follow Ross in using these terms interchangeably. So unless stated otherwise, when I talk of a right act I mean an act that we ought to do, rather than a merely permissible act, and when I talk of what we ought to do, I mean what we morally ought to do, or what is obligatory.

By a *fundamental* moral principle I mean one that is not derived from some other moral principle, and one from which other moral principles are derived. So, for instance, if, as Ross thought, we ought to be honest because by being honest we will be keeping an implicit promise, and we ought to keep our promises, then the principle of fidelity to promises will be fundamental, or at least

Developing Deontology, First Edition. Edited by Brad Hooker. Copyright © 2012 The Authors. Book compilation © 2012 Blackwell Publishing Ltd.

more fundamental, than the principle of honesty. This is because the principle of honesty is derived from that of fidelity. It may be that the principle of fidelity to promises is in turn derived from the principle of good promotion – that we ought to keep our promises when and because we will be producing the best outcome by doing so, and we ought to produce the best outcome. If that is true then fidelity is derivative and good promotion is fundamental.

Derivation here is an explanatory notion. One principle is derived from another if the duty that figures in the derivative principle is explained with reference to the duty that figures in the principle from which it is derived. Note that the notion of derivation here is understood with reference to duties, or obligations, and explanations of these. It is not an epistemological notion of derivation. The fundamental claim here is not that we can *know* that we ought to do a certain sort of act because by doing it we will be doing something else that we ought to do. Rather the claim is that we ought to do the one act because we will be doing something else that we ought to do.

It may be that I can know that I ought to be honest because I know that by being honest I will keep an implicit promise to express my genuine opinions, and I know that I ought to keep my promises. But the order of knowledge need not track the order of explanation of the duties known. For instance a non-derivative moral principle may be knowable with reference to some other principle. That does not mean that the principle known in this way is not really fundamental, or that it is both derivative and non-derivative at the same time. So the fact that some basic moral principle can be known on other grounds and on the basis of our knowledge of other principles, and that our knowledge of the basic principle can be justified with reference to those other grounds and principles in no way casts doubt on its fundamental nature.

Of course, we would expect that what is epistemically fundamental and derivative will track what is explanatorily fundamental and derivative, but it need not do so; and when the epistemic order does track the explanatory order in this respect this will typically be because the relations of grounding and grounded between moral principles are more fundamental than those relating our beliefs in those principles.

What is more fundamental still in this respect is the content of the moral principles rather than the principles themselves. This is because moral principles, at least as I understand them, state that certain acts are right or obligatory, and if one principle is derived from another, this will be because the obligations picked out by one principle are derived from the obligations picked out by the other principle. Relations amongst moral principles simply mirror the relations amongst the obligations they record.

I said at the start that moral principles are those that state prima facie or actual duties. My favoured form of deontology takes its inspiration from W. D. Ross's *The Right and the Good*, so I think the best form of deontology is one spelt out in terms of principles of *prima facie* duty. I favour this form of deontology not just because of doubts about absolutist deontological theories,[1] but more importantly, because principles of prima facie duty are better suited to the task of discovering what is morally fundamental than are principles of duty proper.

I would go so far as to say that basic moral principles *must* be principles of prima facie duty. Principles stated in terms of duty proper can *never* be basic. This is because they all work at the level of what is recommended (peremptorily) – that is, they all state what we ought to do, or are required to do. But in trying to get at what is morally basic we cannot rest content at the level of what is recommended, but have to move to the more fundamental level of what recommends. This level is more fundamental because what recommends explains the relevant recommendation.

If I say to you that you ought to do some act, say, give me £20, it always makes sense for you to ask *why* you ought to do that act.[2] In answering this question I move from the level of what is recommended – your giving me £20 – to the level of what recommends, the reason why you should give me £20. This level is more basic because it explains the recommendation.

It is tempting to say that another ought must figure in the explanation of an ought, and so duties proper, recommendations, must figure in fundamental moral principles. But this cannot be right. For if a duty proper figures in the explanation of some other duty, then we can always ask of the more basic duty *why* we ought

---

[1]   By an absolutist moral theory I mean a theory that holds that there are one or more absolute moral prohibitions – that is, at least one type of act that is always wrong no matter what. Kant is the canonical absolutist, but of course act consequentialists are also absolutists, as they maintain that it is always wrong to fail to promote the good.

[2]   One of the things I find unsatisfactory about moral discourse conducted in terms of rights is that there is no pressure to explain why we have some right.

to do what it recommends, and this will move us back to the fact that recommends rather than to the fact that some action is recommended. To insist that a duty proper must figure in the basic level will lead, therefore, to an infinite regress of explanation.

Since Hume, it is often held that one cannot derive an ought from an is, and so an ought must figure in the explanation of another ought. But we are here talking about explanation, not logical derivation, so even if Hume's principle is true, it is not relevant here. You cannot logically derive an effect from its cause, but that doesn't mean that all causal explanations are deficient.[3] Similarly the fact (assuming it is a fact) that one cannot logically derive an ought from an is doesn't mean that deontic explanations that don't mention oughts are deficient.

As I understand prima facie duties they are recommenders not recommendations. They do not tell you what you should do, but pick out features that give you reason to do certain acts. This point is quite lost in the terminology Ross uses in *The Right and the Good*. But despite the misleading terminology, it is clear that by 'prima facie duty' he does not mean a special sort of duty, or recommendation.[4] He means, rather, a moral feature of acts related to duty proper. The context in which Ross introduces this term, as well as much of what he says about the notion of a prima facie duty, makes it clear that the way in which he thinks that prima facie duties are related to duties proper is by explaining them. Principles of prima facie duty pick out features of acts or situations that tend to make certain acts right. So if they are not defeated in some way they will pick out the reason why some act is right.

This means that principles of prima facie duty pick out explanatory reasons – the *reason why* some act is our duty, or the *reason why*

---

[3]   One might insist that a complete explanation must entail the explanandum, and so some relevant principle must figure in the explanation. This is not the place to dispute this claim. All I'll say is that this is a substantive claim in the theory of explanation, and does not flow from the very idea of explanation. One might think that causal explanations are explanations with reference to causes. On this view a principle could not figure in a causal explanation, as principles do not cause anything, and it is difficult to see how they could be part of a cause of anything.

[4]   "The phase '*prima facie*' duty must be apologized for, since . . . it suggests that what we are speaking of is a certain kind of duty, whereas it is in fact not a duty, but something related in a special way to duty." (W. D. Ross, *The Right and the Good*. Stratton-Lake, P., (ed) (Oxford: Clarendon Press, 2002) p. 20)

we should do that act, or *why* it is right.[5] At this point it may be asked what sort of explanation these facts provide. They clearly do not offer causal explanations. The fact that you have promised to do some act does not cause that act to be obligatory. Neither is this a conceptual, or teleological explanation. But although I can list the sort of explanation that recommenders do *not* stand to the obligations they explain, I have to confess that I cannot offer a positive characterisation of what sort of explanation recommenders provide of deontic facts (though I take some comfort from the fact that no one else has any idea either). What I *can* do, however, is say something about how recommenders relate to normative reasons and motivation. Once we are clear about these connections the task of subsuming something like a Rossian pluralism under some single moral principle in a plausible manner becomes, I suggest, much harder. So my proposal here is that the move from moral principles understood as principles of duty proper, to principles of prima facie duty – from recommendations to recommenders – makes this form of moral pluralism more resistant to subsumption under unifying principles.

I have said the principles of prima facie duty pick out facts that explain why certain acts ought to be done. By facts here I mean instances of properties in certain things or actions, so will sometimes talk of properties, or features, that explain rather than facts. But when I talk of properties in this context I should be taken to mean that some act (or situation or thing) *has* that property – that is, some fact. What gets explained is a distinctive sort of fact – a normative, or more precisely, a deontic fact – the fact that some agent ought (or is required, or is obligated) to do some act. We may call such explanations deontic explanations.

In *Kant, Duty and Moral Worth*[6] I talked of the reasons that figured in deontic explanations as 'the normative reason why I ought to do some act' (see, eg, 18–20). But the phrase 'normative reason why' is an incoherent mixture of two sorts of reasons – a normative reason and an explanatory reason. For some fact to provide a normative reason is for that fact to count in favour of some attitude, or action (or some disjunction or conjunction of

---

[5]   Once again, I am not saying that if these features obtain then we ought to do the relevant act. Rather, if we ought to do the relevant act, then one of these features will be the ultimate explanation why.

[6]   Philip Stratton-Lake, *Kant, Duty, and Moral Worth* (London: Routledge, 2000).

acts or attitudes).[7] I follow Scanlon in thinking of reasons as basic and believe that all we can say about the way in which these facts count in favour of attitudes and actions is that they do so by providing a reason.[8]

I have said that deontic explanations are facts that explain deontic facts. The explainers are the *reasons why* these deontic facts obtain. So the explainers are a certain sort of reason. But they are explanatory, not normative reasons – they are the *reasons why* we ought to do some act, and 'the reason why' is an explanatory reason.

Although I do not know how to argue for this view, I believe that every such explanatory reason is also a normative reason.[9] The reason that explains why we ought to do some act is always a normative reason to do that act. Or to put this another way:

If F explains why you ought to Φ, then F gives you a reason to Φ

So, for instance, if you ought to Φ because you promised to, then the fact that you promised to Φ gives you a reason to Φ. Or if you ought to Φ because Φing will prevent a great deal of suffering, then the fact that Φing will prevent a great deal of suffering gives you a reason to Φ. And so on. This link between explanatory and normative reasons is, I think, why I conflated these two notions in *Kant, Duty, and Moral Worth*. But although the explanatory and the normative reason are the same fact, the normative reason does not count in favour of the same thing that the explanatory reason explains. The explanatory reason explains the fact that I ought to do some act. It is a relation between the fact F and this deontic fact. The normative reason is provided by the same (explanatory) fact F, but does not count in favour of the deontic fact. It could not, for deontic facts are not the sort of thing of which normative

---

[7] Scanlon insists that they count in favour only of attitudes (See T. M. Scanlon, *What We Owe to Each Other* (Cambridge, Massachusetts: Harvard University Press, 1998) p. 21), but that causes unnecessary complications.

[8] *What We Owe to Each Other*, p. 17.

[9] John Broome, also endorses this principle in his 'Reasons' in *Reason and Value: Themes from the Moral Philosophy of Joseph Raz*. R. Jay Wallace, Philip Pettit, Samuel Scheffler, and Michael Smith (Eds). (Oxford: Clarendon Press, 2006) pp. 28–55.

reasons can count in favour. What F counts in favour of is not the fact that I ought to do a certain act, but my doing this act.[10]

So by replacing principles of duty proper with principles of prima facie duty we move away from principles telling us what we ought to do to principles that state which facts are the *reasons why* we ought to do certain acts, and which provide us with reasons to do those acts. Because of their essential connection with obligations we may call these reasons *moral* reasons, and it is less confusing if we call the principles that specify these reasons *principles of moral reasons* rather than principles of prima facie duty.

Deontic Reasons

There is a tendency amongst Kantians, as well as other philosophers, to regard the obligation itself as the distinctive moral reason, but this cannot be the only moral reason we have, as Kant himself seemed to think, and once we recognise that facts that provide deontic explanations are moral reasons, the temptation to think that such deontic facts are any sort of normative reason should diminish. We always have a moral reason to do what we ought to do, not because the fact that we ought to do that act is a reason, but because the fact that explains this deontic fact is a reason. Once we are aware of the reasons provided by the facts that explain our obligations, it will seem very odd to suppose that the obligations themselves are also reason providing.

Suppose I tell you that you ought to be grateful to Brad, and you ask 'why?'. I reply by pointing to the various things Brad has done for you in the past, often at some cost to himself, and claim

---

[10]   At this point it is worth noting an ambiguity in the notion of a normative reason. It can mean either the fact that provides the normative reason, or the fact that that fact provides a normative reason. We may, following Parfit, call the first a normatively significant fact and the second a normative fact. Understood as normatively significant facts, normative reasons are the facts that stand in the reason providing relation to some attitude or action. Understood as a normative fact, a normative reason is the relation the first fact stands to the relevant attitude or action.

This ambiguity will be important in getting clear about whether what explains deontic facts is the same reason we have to do what we ought to do, as the answer is that in one way it is, and in another it is not. The explanatory reason *is* the normative reason, where the latter is understood as the normatively significant fact: But it is not the normative reason if it is understood as the normative fact. The fact that F is a reason for me to do some act is not the same as the fact that F is the reason why I ought to do that act. But the fact that explains what I ought to do and which is a reason for me to do what I ought to do is the same.

that you ought to be grateful to him for that reason. Given the principled link between deontic explanations and moral reasons, by telling you the *reason why* you ought to be grateful I have, at the same time, picked out facts that give you a *normative* reason to be grateful. Let's assume you accept this. So you know that the various favours that Brad has done for you in the past not only explain why you ought to be grateful, but also give you a moral reason to be grateful. It is hard to imagine that you might ever be tempted to say that I have not listed all of the moral reasons you have to be grateful – that I have left out a, if not the most important, moral reason to be grateful – namely, the fact that I ought to be grateful. The only reason I can think why someone might insist that this deontic fact is reason providing is that they cannot think of where else the distinctively *moral* reason to act could be located. Once we see clearly that this may plausibly be located in the facts that figure in the deontic explanation, the temptation to think that distinctively *moral* reasons must be provided by the deontic fact should at least diminish. I think they disappear.

Moral reasons and moral motivation.

So far I have talked about a certain type of explanatory reason – the one that figures in deontic explanations – and the normative reason the explanatory reason provides to comply with the obligation it explains. But there is a third sort of reason that is closely linked to the first two, which is a motivational reason. So it is to this, and the relation it stands to the explanatory and normative reasons discussed so far, that I now turn.

In one of her papers Christine Korsgaard makes the following claim about Kant's argument for the Categorical Imperative in *Groundwork* I:

> Kant is analysing the good will, characterised as one that does what is right because it is right, in order to discover the principle of unconditionally good action. The assumption behind such an analysis is that *the reason why a good-willed person does an action, and the reason why the action is right, are the same.*[11]

[11] 'Kant's Analysis of Obligation', in *Creating the Kingdom of Ends* (Cambridge: Cambridge University Press, 1996, pp. 43–76) p. 60.

Although I think that this assumption has to be hedged by various conditions,[12] I think it is true – that morally good people will tend to be motivated to do what they ought to do by the reasons why they ought to do those acts. Since this thesis asserts a symmetry between the facts that explain why we ought to act in certain ways and why good people tend act in those ways, I call this the symmetry thesis.

Gripped by the Kantian view that the thought of duty is the only thing that will motivate good people, Korsgaard also claims that '[t]he good-willed individual does the right thing because it is the right thing', but given the symmetry thesis this cannot be correct. For if they do the right thing for the reason why it is right, and they do the right thing because it was right, it would follow that the right act is right because it is right, and that, of course, is no explanation at all.

Given that the facts that explain why we ought to do certain acts give us a moral reason to do those acts, it is no surprise that the symmetry thesis is true, at least once it is freed from Kantian prejudices about moral motivation. For all it states is that virtuous individuals will be motivated to do what they morally ought to do by the moral reasons they have for doing those acts, which is just what we would expect from the practically wise.

Indirect consequentialists will object to the symmetry thesis on the ground that it rules out a view they endorse. Indirect consequentialists might hold that we are unlikely to perform the acts that will produce the best outcome if we are motivated only by consequentialst considerations. For various reasons the best outcome is much more likely to be produced if we do not always aim to bring about the best outcome. It may be produced by a motivational set that treated non-consequentialist considerations as moral reasons – not merely as derivative reasons, but as reasons on their own account. So such consequentialists may have motivations which are indistinguishable from those of Rossian deontologists. If this form of consequentialism were correct, then the features that would motivate good people to do what they ought to do would *not* be the same as the reasons why they ought to do those acts, and the symmetry thesis would be false.

But that indirect consequentialists would reject the symmetry thesis does not seem to me to cause a serious problem for the thesis. This is in no small part because the symmetry thesis has a great deal

---

[12] See my *Kant, Duty, and Moral Worth*, pp. 16–20.

of initial plausibility to it and a rationale that is independent of any particular normative theory. If you are motivated by some consideration it seems you must regard that consideration as a reason to act, and in so far as you are rational we would expect you to be motivated by what you regard as reasons to act. A normative theory that requires us to be motivated to do what we ought to do by anything other than the reasons why we ought to do those acts requires that we sever this link between our normative judgements and the explanation of our actions. That counts against the normative theory rather than against the symmetry thesis.

Furthermore, it is not even clear that such a severance is psychologically possible. Could we persuade ourselves that non-consequentialist reasons have no independent normative force, and gain any normative force they have only by association with consequentialist considerations, and, at the same time, get ourselves to be motivated *non-derivatively* by these non-consequentialist considerations? It would seem that the only way in which we could get ourselves to be non-derivatively motivated by non-consequentialist considerations is to regard those considerations as providing non-derivative reasons. But we could not get ourselves to believe that while we believe consequentialism.

For both these reasons I think that the fact that some normative theory requires us to reject the symmetry thesis should cast doubt on that theory rather than the symmetry thesis with which it is incompatible.[13]

Furthermore, in so far as some theory requires us to reject the symmetry thesis, it will complicate the connections between the three moral reasons so far mentioned – namely, the reasons why we morally ought to do certain acts, the moral reasons we have to do them, and the reasons why good people will do them. The Rossian view simply identifies these reasons in an economical, elegant and plausible manner. By rejecting this economical and elegant symmetry a monistic theory like consequentialism undermines at least some of the supposed advantage it has over pluralistic theories by having a single grounding principle. A theory with a single grounding principle is, all other things being equal,

---

[13] There are many other criticisms of consequentialist attempts to separate motivation and justification. See especially "Indirect Consequentialism, Friendship, and the Problem of Alienation" by Dean Cocking and Justin Oakley. (*Ethics*, Vol. 106, No. 1 (Oct., 1995), pp. 86–111)

better than one with more basic principles, because it is simpler.[14] But if this gain in simplicity generates further complications elsewhere, it is not at all clear that there is an overall gain in theoretical simplicity, such that the monist theory is, in this respect, a better theory than the pluralist one.

Being wronged and reasons to resent

I now turn to a fourth and final reason that the facts picked out by basic principles of prima facie duty provide. These facts are the ones that pick out whom we have wronged when we wrong someone, and the feature in virtue of which we have wronged them. For someone to be wronged by my action is for that person to have reason to resent my action. The feature in virtue of which this person is wronged is the fact that provides this reason.

Arguably at least, not all wrong acts involve wronging someone. If, for instance, I drive home drunk without having an accident, then it seems I have acted wrongly without wronging anyone. For although everyone would have reason to disapprove of my reckless behaviour, I do not think that anyone would have reason to resent it. Nevertheless, most wrong acts involve wronging certain individuals or groups. If I fail to keep my promise to you, then I not only act wrongly, but also wrong *you*. If I fail to be grateful to someone who did me a favour in the past, then I wrong that person, and if I fail to save someone whom I could easily help, without any significant cost to myself, then I wrong that person by ignoring his plight.[15]

---

[14] Brad Hooker makes much of this in his argument for rule-consequentialism in his *Ideal Code, Real World: A Rule-Consequentialist Theory of Morality* (Oxford: Clarendon Press, 2000), pp. 19–23.

[15] It is often said that we only wrong the other person if they have a right against us, and that this is not the case in relation to beneficence. Accident victims, or the starving or destitute, have no right to our help, so, it is claimed, we do not wrong them when we fail to help. We may question this claim. We do not need to attribute a right to be helped to ground the claim that in failing to help them we wrong them. All we need is the idea that we owe help to others in such cases, and we do not need to assume that the needy have a right to be helped to ground that idea. It may be sufficient for an act of help to be owed to another person or group for us to be unable to justify not helping on grounds the other person could not reasonably reject. And we could not justify our failure to help someone in dire need when helping would involve little effort on our part. Suppose, to use a variant of Scanlon's example, you are trapped under some electrical equipment, and you are receiving agonizing electrical shocks as a result. I am walking by and notice that I could end your suffering by flicking the fuse switch nearby. It is impossible to imagine that I could justify my failing to press the switch to you on grounds you could not reasonably reject.

One of the virtues of a Rossian theory of prima facie duty, or as I prefer to call them, principles of moral reasons, is that the facts picked out by these principles not only give us moral reason to act in certain ways, explain why we ought to act in those ways, and explain why we act in those ways (in so far as we were virtuous), but also pick out the individuals or groups who are wronged if we fail to act in those ways. They also pick out the features in virtue of which those individuals are wronged.

Ross maintains that the reason why I ought to keep my promise to A to do a certain act is simply that I have promised A that I would do that act; and the reason why I ought to be grateful to B is that B benefited me in the past. These reasons are captured in the principles of fidelity and gratitude. The principle of fidelity states that the fact that I have promised A to Φ gives me a moral reason to Φ, and the principle of gratitude states that the fact that B did me a favour in the past gives me a reason to be grateful to B. Assuming that these reasons are not defeated, it will turn out that my duty proper is to keep my promise, or be grateful, and the facts mentioned in these principles will explain these duties. Since it is the fact that I promised *A* that explains my obligation to do what I have promised, it is A who is wronged if I fail to keep my promise. Since it is the fact that *B* benefited me in the past that explains my obligation to be grateful to *B*, it is B who is wronged if I miss an opportunity to express my gratitude to B, or reciprocate. It is A and B in each case who have reason to resent my not doing what I promised to do and my failure to be grateful respectively.

Being wronged is not the same as being harmed here. My promise to A may be to help B, and my failure to help B may be something that does not harm A in any way. It may, therefore, be the case that I harm B by breaking my promise. In such a case I wrong A, not B, even though it is B who is harmed and not A, for it is to A that I promised to help B. Similarly, when I fail to benefit B when I ought to, I will wrong him, but I need not harm him. Failing to benefit someone is not harming them. I could benefit all of my students now by giving each of them a five pound note, but I am not harming them by not doing this.

That would make my helping you in this way something I owe to you. This in turn would be sufficient warrant the claim that by failing to press the fuse switch I not only act wrongly, but wrong you.

Principles of moral reasons also pick out the reason an individual has to resent my failure to do what I ought. These features are the same as the reason why I ought to do the acts I failed to do. In relation to A it is the fact that I promised him that I would do a certain act, and in relation to B it is the fact that he did me a favour in the past. In the first case, the reason A has to resent my failure to do a certain act is provided by the fact that I promised A that I would do that act. In the case of B's resenting my not benefiting him, the reason to resent my failure is provided by the fact that he benefited me in the past. In each case the reason why I ought to do a certain act, the reason I have to do that act, and the reason another person has to resent my not doing that act are provided by the same facts – the facts picked out by the principles of moral reasons.

To summarise then: the best form of deontology is defined in terms of a plurality of principles of moral reasons. Each of these principles picks out four reasons – two normative and two explanatory. If F is the feature that is prima facie right, and succeeds in making Φing my duty proper, then:

1. F is the reason why I ought to Φ.
2. F is a moral reason for me to Φ.
3. F will be a reason why I Φ, in so far as I am virtuous.
4. F will be a reason for those wronged by my not Φing to resent my not Φing.

So although there is a plurality of basic moral principles in this Rossian deontology, these principles do give us an elegant and very simple account of these four moral reasons. Given that any moral theory, in so far as it aims to provide the fundamental moral principles or principle, should provide principles of this form – that is, principles that pick out recommenders rather than simply provide recommendations – any attempt to reduce a Rossian pluralism to a single principle of moral reasons must pick out a single feature that provides a plausible account of all four reasons. At the very least a failure to do so will be a strong pro tanto consideration against the reductive theory, for in this respect it will have lost much of the simplicity the Rossian theory has, despite the gain in simplicity gained by the reduction itself. Rossian pluralism is resistant to such reductions because no single principle can pick out a single feature that provides a plausible account of all four reasons for every action that we ought to do.

Moral reasons and recalcitrant pluralism

It is much more plausible to subsume a plurality of moral principles under a single principle if these principles are principles of duty proper. This is because the recommendations contained in what will become the derivative principles will remain in place, and will simply be explained by some other recommendation, such as the recommendation to produce as much intrinsic value as possible. So the principle telling me to keep my promises is left untouched if grounded by a principle telling me to do this because by doing it I will be complying with a principle telling me to do something else, like maximise the good. But it is much harder to present a plausible monistic reduction if we are starting with principles of moral reasons. This is because the facts picked out by these principles must be able to be reasons in the four different ways I have outlined above.

What I want to do now is briefly illustrate how this form of deontological pluralism makes it harder to subsume the plurality of basic moral principles under a single principle in a plausible way by showing how it deals with a particular subsumptive strategy employed by consequentialists. The particular strategy I have in mind is that of 'expanding the good'. I'll focus on Robert Shaver's attempt to employ this strategy as he focuses on Prichard's and Ross's anti-consequentialist arguments.

Expanding the good

So what is the 'expanding the good' strategy? It's basically a set of simple instructions on how to absorb any apparent counter-example to consequentialism. The instructions are as follows:

1) For any supposed counter example to consequentialism, such as a case where some special personal relation seems to make a moral difference on its own account, take the act that constitutes honouring or respecting that relationship.
2) Treat the fact that this act occurred as a consequence of the act.
3) Maintain that that consequence has intrinsic value.
4) Maintain that it is the intrinsic value of this consequence that accounts for, and thus neutralises the apparent counter-example to consequentialism.

By following these instructions, it is argued, consequentialism can get the right answer to these difficult cases.

There are two standard objections to this strategy. The first is to maintain that this strategy achieves only a semantic victory for consequentialism, so is really just an empty move. The other is to claim that this strategy gives rise to the wrong sort of moral motivation. I have argued that normative moral theories are best understood as theories of moral reasons on the ground that such principles are best suited to the job of finding foundational moral principles. So understood the expanding the good strategy is not merely an empty move, but makes a substantive claim, and in my view is mistaken. The moral motivation point is correct as far as it goes, but picks up on only one of the four moral reasons picked out by such principles, and can be bolstered by the other ways in which the content of basic moral principles picks out moral reasons.

Family relations

In "What is the Basis of Moral Obligation?" Prichard gets us to consider the following scenario:

> Suppose all the houses and provisions of a village are damaged by a landslide, and suppose every villager but one is hurt. Suppose the circumstances such that the one sound man could only devote himself to providing food and shelter for one person. The acquisition of food and shelter by each would be equally good. Hence on the [ideal utilitarian] view there would be an obligation and an equal obligation on the one sound man to find food and shelter for himself, for his parent, and for a stranger. But while it might be contended that he had the right to consider himself as much as any other . . . no one would suppose that he was under a positive obligation to do so. Moreover everyone would hold, contrary to the view, that the obligation to help his father was greater than that to help a stranger.[16]

In his "The Birth of Deontology"[17] Shaver argues that an ideal utilitarian may try to deal with this type of objection by expanding

---

[16] "What is the Basis of Moral Obligation?", in *Moral Writings*, Jim MacAdam (ed). Oxford: Oxford University Press, 2002) p. 2.

[17] In *Underivative Duty: British Moral Philosophers from Sidgwick to Ewing*. Thomas Hurka (ed). (Oxford: Oxford University Press, 2010), pp. 126–45.

the good. Prichard's objection seems to treat human well-being as the only good. It is on this ground that he thinks that the utilitarian would claim that the villager ought to help either himself, his father, or the stranger, as the benefit to each of them is the same. But, Shaver points out, ideal utilitarians need not be restricted in this way. They can allow that many other things are good. They could allow that a state of affairs in which a son helps his father is intrinsically good, and the intrinsic value of a state in which a son helps his father would enable the ideal utilitarian to claim that in the situation Prichard describes the villager ought to help his father rather than the stranger. This is because the good consequence 'that a son helps his father' breaks the tie between the other goods provided by the equal benefits he can confer either on his father, the stranger, or himself.

So the ideal utilitarian is not committed to saying that in such situations the villager ought to help either his father, the stranger, or himself. Rather, ideal utilitarianism can generate the more plausible answer – namely, that the he ought to help his father, and would have acted wrongly if he benefited the stranger.

Shaver puts his point as one about what one ought to do. His concern was to show that the ideal utilitarian would recommend the right action in cases where personal relations seem relevant. But as a contribution to the debate about fundamental normative theory he would have to claim not only that the villager should help his father in preference to a stranger, but that the reason why he should do this is because by doing so he will bring about an intrinsically better state of affairs than any other action open to him. But if this is the reason why the villager ought to save his father, it would also have to be the reason for the villager to save his father, the reason why he would save his father (in so far as he is virtuous), and the reason his father would have to resent his son's action if he helped the stranger, or did nothing.

The son's motive

I think the fact that the act will produce the best outcome fails to provide a satisfactory account of any of these reasons. In defending this view I shall start with the villager's motivating reason. Let us suppose that the villager is a decent individual who aims to do not only the right thing, but also for the right reason. Let us also assume that his judgement about such matters is good and so he typically succeeds in doing the right thing for the right reason. So he rightly judges that he should help his father. Why would he help his father in preference to a stranger? Given the symmetry thesis this will be because of the reason why he ought to help his father. So if the consequentialist account of why he ought to help his father is correct, then the reason why he would help him in preference to a stranger would be because he will be producing a better state of affairs in the world than if he did any other act. The fact that he stands in any special relation to his father would not count at all; for according to consequentialism, the reason why he should help his father in preference to a stranger is not because he stands in this relation – that is the deontologist's answer – but because by doing this he will be bringing about an intrinsically better state of affairs.

The deciding factor in whether this state of affairs is best is the fact that his act will have as a consequence a state in which a son helps his father. But this should not lead us to think that the relation that figures in this state will figure in the villager's motivation after all. The fact that his act will have this consequence is the reason why the act will have the best outcome, since it breaks the tie between the value of the benefit conferred on either his father, or a stranger. But it is the fact that his act has produced the best outcome, not the fact that it has produced a state in which a son helps a father, that makes it the right act to do. Otherwise this really would look like a mere semantic victory for the consequentialist. What makes it stand out from the intuitionist account is that it is the production of impartial value that grounds this duty. This is not merely a rewording of the intuitionists view.

But it is very hard to accept that the son would be motivated by a concern to produce impartial value in so far as he is virtuous. If asked why he helped his father instead of the stranger he would, I would suggest, answer 'because he is my father'. His answer would be the same if we asked him why he thought he *should* help his father instead of the stranger. The reason why he would help, and his view about the reason why he should help, his father would be the same, and neither would mention the amount of intrinsic value that his act would produce.

Shaver is aware of this objection to the expanding the good strategy. He writes,

[someone] might reply that the problem is not that the ideal utilitarian cites consequences too far removed from those we

really cite. It is rather that in deciding upon our duty, we do not think of these states of affairs as goods at all. But while this may be sometimes, or even often, true, the ideal utilitarian can note that if, on reflection, we do think these states of affairs are goods, it does not matter much that we do not in every instance of acting have this thought.[18]

But it does matter. The motivating thoughts of good people typically reveal what they regard as the features that explain why they ought to act in certain ways. As far as that goes it is just irrelevant whether on reflection the villager comes to recognize that helping his father would bring about the best state of affairs. The villager could accept that in helping his father he would be bringing about a state of affairs in which a son helps his father (how could he deny that!), and may also accept that this state is intrinsically good. This in no way supports consequentialism over deontology. For a start he may think that this state of affairs is good because it is one in which the son has done what he ought to do. Then the duty would explain the goodness, rather than the goodness explain the duty; and the duty would have to be explained on other grounds.

Furthermore, although the villager might accept that his act will have a good consequence, it is difficult to imagine that this would get him to revise his initial account of why he ought to help his father – that is, of what really matters to him here. What matters to the villager, and what will motivate him to act, is that he would be helping his father, not that by doing so he would be making the world a better place. And if this fact about his father motivates him to do what he should, even after reflection, this shows that he regards this fact as a reason to do what he should.

Things are worse when we turn to the reasons for resentment. Suppose that the villager helped the stranger instead of his father, perhaps because he thought that he would produce the same amount of good either way and decided to settle the issue by tossing a coin. His father would then have reason to resent

---

[18] 'Prichard's Arguments Against Ideal Utilitarianism', in *Partiality and Impartiality, Vol. II*. Brian Feltham and Philip Stratton-Lake (eds) (Oxford: Oxford University Press, forthcoming). Shaver notes that Ross recognises this point in his *Foundations of Ethics* (Oxford: Clarendon Press, 1939) p. 69.

the fact that his son helped a stranger in preference to his father. What would provide this reason? If the consequentialist answer were correct then it would have to be the fact that his son failed to produce the intrinsically best state of affairs. But although that *could* be the reason for his father (and for anyone else) for that matter, to *disapprove* of his son's action, that could not be the reason for his father to resent his son's action. On the contrary, the fact that the villager has failed to bring about the best state of affairs leaves the fact that his father has been wronged completely unexplained. If anyone is wronged here, it would be the world which has not been made as good as it could have been. But that, of course, makes no sense.

Shaver also tries the same strategy in relation to cases where keeping a promise seems to mean that the right act is not the one with the best consequences. Exactly the same objections would apply to this instance of the expanding the good strategy as applied to the case of the villager helping his father.

Indeed, once we see that Ross's principles of prima facie duty are principles of moral reasons in the four different ways mentioned, even Ross's own attempt to reduce the principles of justice, self-improvement and beneficence to the principle of promoting the good looks unlikely to succeed.

Other, non-consequentialist monistic theories might do better. For instance an attempt to subsume all of Ross's basic principles under a Kantian principle of respecting others as ends in themselves might be able to provide a plausible account of the four moral reasons mentioned. But whether it does will depend on how the idea of treating others as ends in themselves is understood. If we take Kant seriously when he equates this principle with the principle of universalizability it looks hopeless. And Robert Audi's interpretation of treating others as ends in themselves looks too close to treating others beneficently to free itself from variants of Ross's criticisms of utilitarian reductions, especially if the principle of beneficence is subsumed under the principle of promoting the good.[19]

But even if other monistic theories do better than consequentialism in providing a plausible account of the four moral reasons

---

[19] See Audi's *The Good in the Right, A Theory of Intuition and Intrinsic Value* (Princeton: Princeton University Press, 2004) pp. 91–2.

mentioned here, my claim is that a Rossian understanding of moral principles as principles of moral reasons makes it much harder for monistic theories to succeed in their reductions. So even if some monistic theories can overcome this extra difficulty, I hope at least to persuade you that there is this extra difficulty to overcome.

3

DEFENDING DOUBLE EFFECT

Ralph Wedgwood

Abstract
This essay defends a version of the Doctrine of Double Effect (DDE) – the doctrine that there is normally a stronger reason against an act that has a bad state of affairs as one of its intended effects than against an otherwise similar act that has that bad state of affairs as an unintended effect. First, a precise account of this version of the DDE is given. Secondly, some suggestions are made about why we should believe the DDE, and about why it is true. Finally, a solution is developed to the so-called 'closeness problem' that any version of the DDE must face.

0. One form of deontological ethics involves the so-called Doctrine of Double Effect (DDE).[1] As I shall interpret it here, the DDE is the thesis that there is normally a *stronger* reason against an act if that act has a bad state of affairs (like an innocent person's death) as one of its *intended* effects than if that bad state of affairs is merely one of the act's *unintended* effects. In short, according to the DDE, it is harder to justify an act that has a bad effect if that effect is intended than if it is not intended.

Many writers have criticized the DDE.[2] In this essay, I shall offer a partial defence, by giving a precise account of one version of the doctrine, and answering some of the objections that have been raised against it.

1. The version of the DDE that I shall defend here is not exactly identical to the versions that have been discussed by other philosophers. For example, consider the version of the DDE that is discussed by T. M. Scanlon (2009, 1):

---

[1]   The doctrine goes back at least as far as Thomas Aquinas's discussion of self-defence; see *Summa Theologica*, IIa IIae, 64, 7.

[2]   Notably, the DDE has been criticized by some proponents of deontological ethics, such as Judith Thomson (1991 and 1999) and T. M. Scanlon (2009). I have already responded, at least briefly, to their objections elsewhere; see Wedgwood (2011). This is why I shall focus on different objections here.

Developing Deontology, First Edition. Edited by Brad Hooker. Copyright © 2012 The Authors. Book compilation © 2012 Blackwell Publishing Ltd.

The doctrine of double effect holds that an action that aims at the death of an innocent person, either as its end or as a means to its end, is always wrong.

There are several differences between Scanlon's version of the doctrine and the version that I shall defend here. First, Scanlon's version condemns all acts that 'aim at' the death of an innocent person, regardless of whether these acts succeeding in achieving this aim or not. The version of the DDE that I shall defend here, by contrast, concerns only those acts that *succeed* in realizing the bad state of affairs that they were aiming at. In my view, acts that aim at a bad state of affairs but *fail* to achieve this aim fall into a somewhat different category – which unfortunately I shall not have time to discuss here.

Secondly, the version of the doctrine that Scanlon discusses is narrowly focused on acts that aim at the *death of an innocent person.* But it seems clear that if this version of the doctrine is true, this will not be because of anything special about *deaths* in particular; instead it will be because of a fundamental difference between the roles of intended effects and unintended effects in generating reasons against action. For this reason, I shall focus on a significantly broader version of the doctrine here, which is concerned with all acts that have a *bad state of affairs* among their intended effects. My version can presumably explain the more restricted version that is concerned solely with deaths, since an innocent person's death is presumably normally a 'bad state of affairs' in the relevant sense.

As I shall sometimes put it, when one intends a state of affairs that is bad in the relevant way, one's intention is a 'bad intention'; and when one intends a state of affairs that is not bad in this way, one's intention is an innocent or permissible intention. So another way to put the central idea of the DDE is by saying that at least normally, other things being equal, there is a stronger reason against an act that is the successful execution of a bad intention than against an otherwise similar act that is the execution of an innocent or permissible intention.

Finally, there is another crucial difference between Scanlon's version of the DDE and mine. Scanlon's version is *absolutist*: it implies that acts that have an innocent person's death as one of their intended effects are *always* wrong. But Warren Quinn's (1989) version of the doctrine seems more plausible: according to Quinn's version, the fact that an act has a bad state of affairs as one of its intended effects normally *strengthens* the reason *against* the act, but it does not *invariably* make the act *impermissible* (since sufficiently strong countervailing reasons may make the act permissible after all).

The central claim of my version of the DDE, then, is that there is normally a stronger reason against an act if the act has a bad state of affairs as one of its intended effects than if it has that bad state of affairs as one of its unintended effects. Bad intended effects count more strongly against actions than bad unintended effects. Moreover, the difference in strength between these two reasons against acting is non-trivial: at least sometimes this difference can make it the case that an act that is done with a bad intention is impermissible, while an otherwise exactly similar act that is done with an innocent intention is permissible.

There are some further questions about how exactly to interpret the doctrine that need to be addressed before proceeding. First, what is meant here by an 'effect' of an act? I shall use the term broadly here, so that an 'effect' of an act comes to exactly the same thing as a 'consequence' of the act: it is simply a state of affairs that would obtain if the act were to be performed, but might not obtain if the act were not performed.[3]

Secondly, what do I mean by saying that some consequences of an action are 'bad'? The sort of badness that I have in mind here is an *agent-neutral* sort of badness. A state of affairs that is 'bad' in this agent-neutral way is not just *bad for me* (which might be compatible with its being good for everyone else), but bad in a way that makes it appropriate for *everyone* to regret or lament the state of affairs (regardless of who they are, or how precisely they are related to this state of affairs). There is much more that could be said about this idea of the agent-neutral badness of states of affairs; but I shall not pursue these issues here. For the purposes of this discussion, I shall have to rely on an intuitive grasp of this sort of agent-neutral badness. However, I have *not* said that when

---

[3] Following David Lewis (1973), I assume here that the 'might'-counterfactual 'If it were the case that *p*, it *might not* be the case that *q*' is equivalent to the negation of the 'would'-counterfactual 'If it were the case that *p*, it would be the case that *q*'. The consequences of an act need not always be states of affairs that *would not* obtain if the act were not performed. Suppose that there are three available acts, *A*, *B*, and *C*, and a state of affairs *S*, such that *A* and *B* would each result in *S*'s obtaining, while *C* would result in *S*'s not obtaining. Then it would not be true that if you were not to do *A*, *S* would not obtain (since if you did not do *A*, you might do *B* – in which case *S* would still obtain); but *S* surely still counts as a consequence of *A*.

a state of affairs is bad in the relevant way, that state of affairs is *intrinsically* bad. I have left it open that the states of affairs that are bad in the relevant way may be merely *extrinsically* rather than intrinsically bad. (We shall return to this point when we discuss the 'closeness problem' for the DDE in the last section of this paper.)

Thirdly, we also need to clarify our talk of 'acts' and 'actions'. One crucial distinction is between act-types and act-tokens.[4] An act-token is a particular act that is actually performed by a particular agent at a particular time. By contrast, an act-type can be performed on many different occasions, and by many different agents. Moreover, an act-type can exist even if it is never actually performed – the most that is required for the existence of an act-type is the *possibility* of there being a performance of that type.

Given my interpretation of the DDE, the kind of judgments that we need to focus on here are judgments about the strength of an agent's reasons for or against various available actions – including actions that the agent never actually performs. It seems that these are most naturally taken as judgments on *act-types*, considered as possible options for a particular agent in a particular choice situation. For example, the statement 'There is a reason for you to call your mother tomorrow' states that there is a certain relation (the reason-for relation) between *you*, an *act-type* (calling your mother) and an *occasion* (tomorrow).

Here, however, there is a complication that we need to take account of. Some act-types are more *specific* and *detailed* than others. For example, the act of flying from Mexico to Toronto is a more specific act-type than the act of flying somewhere in North America: it is necessary that anyone who does the first act also does the second, but not *vice versa*. Similarly the acts that are, intuitively, proper parts of other acts – as covering the distance from Mexico to the US border is part of the act of travelling the whole distance from Mexico to Toronto – are also less specific than the acts of which they are proper parts, since here again, it is possible to do the former act without doing the latter but not *vice versa*.

One way in which an act-type can be more specific than another is if the more specific type itself contains a specific intention.

---

[4]   This terminology has now become standard, but it was first used in this way by Alvin Goldman (1970), alluding to the well-known distinction between *linguistic* types and tokens.

Thus, in the famous trolley case that was originally due to Philippa Foot (1978, 23), one relatively general act-type might be *diverting the runaway trolley onto the side track*; but there are also two more specific act-types, each of which incorporates a specific intention with which one might divert the trolley – *diverting the trolley in order to kill the person on the side track*, and *diverting the trolley in order to save the five people on the main track*. I shall call the act-types that do not incorporate the intention in this way the 'thin' act-types, while the act-types that do incorporate the intention in this way will be called the 'thick' act-types.

Fundamentally, as I am interpreting it, the DDE is concerned with the *thick* act-types, such as *diverting the trolley in order to kill the person on the side track*, and *diverting the trolley in order to save the five people on the main track*. The central claim of the DDE, as I shall interpret it, is that there is normally a stronger reason against a thick act-type that involves successfully executing a bad intention (that is, an intention to bring about a state of affairs that is bad in the relevant way) than an otherwise similar act-type that involves executing innocent intentions instead.

Finally, we need to make it clearer what we mean here by an 'intention'. Much of the literature on the DDE is deplorably unclear about this. In particular, it is crucial to distinguish between (i) the intention with which the action is performed, and (ii) the motivation that lies behind and explains the intention. The motivation of an action consists of the whole of the mental process that terminates in the action; this process typically includes many mental states in addition to intentions – such as desires, emotions, wishes, and beliefs (including of course normative and evaluative beliefs). Within this process, the intentions are in a sense the *last* purely mental component immediately preceding the action; and the action itself just *is* the execution of the intention. In this sense, the agent's intention in acting is no mere *antecedent* of the act, but an essential constituent of the act itself.

The crucial feature of an intention, then, which differentiates it from the other mental states that are involved in the motivation of action, is that the act itself *is* the execution of the intention. Executing an intention involves behaving in a way that is *guided* and *controlled* by that intention. Consider, for example, your intention to make an omelette. This intention consists in a conception of a possible causal sequence of events that might take place, one after another (breaking and beating some eggs, melting some butter in a frying pan, and so on), such that this sequence of events will result in your making an omelette. In executing this intention, you will be constantly monitoring events as they unfold in your kitchen, and constantly adjusting your behaviour in such a way as to ensure that the actual sequence of events conforms to this conception.[5]

Since the fundamental role of an intention is to guide or regulate the agent's voluntary behaviour, the content of an intention always concerns events that the agent takes to be within her power to control. So, for example, if you place a bomb on an aeroplane, in order to destroy some incriminating documents that are on the plane, your intention is to blow up the whole plane and all its contents, since you know perfectly well that this course of action cannot exercise any control over the documents except through acting on the plane and all its contents.

The version of the DDE that I shall defend here concerns intentions in this strict sense of the term. It does *not* concern the agent's motives in general. I shall take no stand on whether all of the agent's motives make a difference to the permissibility of the action. The only doctrine that I shall defend is the thesis that – whatever the agent's other motives may be – there is a stronger reason against an act that has a bad state of affairs as one of its *intended* effects than against an otherwise similar act that has that bad state of affairs as one of its *unintended* effects.

Even though I have in this way restricted the version of the DDE that I am considering, so that it concerns only intentions in this strict sense of the term, it is still a strong and controversial doctrine. First, I have generalized the doctrine so that it covers *all* cases in which a bad state of affairs is intended, not just intentional killings. Secondly, the doctrine implies that intentions have *intrinsic* or *non-derivative* ethical significance. There is a stronger reason against bringing about bad effects through executing an intention to do so than against bringing about such bad effects without intending to precisely *because* of the difference that consists in the presence or absence of this intention. The greater strength of the reason against acting is not explained by something that is merely correlated with the intention, but by the intention itself.

So far, I have focused on the thick act-types, like *diverting the trolley in order to kill the person on the side track*, and *diverting the trolley*

⁵   For some particularly illuminating discussions of intention, see Bratman (1987) and Mele (2000).

in order to save the five people on the main track. As I have explained, the DDE implies that there could be cases in which the first of these two thick act-types is impermissible, while the second thick act-type is permissible. That is, there could be cases in which it is impermissible to divert the trolley in order to kill the person on the side track, but permissible to divert the trolley in order to save the five people on the main track; indeed, in some cases of this sort, it might even be true that you *ought* to divert the trolley onto the side track in order to save the five on the main track (although of course you ought not do it in order to kill the one person on the side track).

However, what should the DDE say about the *thin* act-types, like simply *diverting the trolley*? Presumably, philosophers who follow the 'actualist' view of Frank Jackson and Robert Pargetter (1986) will assume that proponents of the DDE must say that a thin act-type is permissible only if the agent *would* do it with a permissible intention *if he did it.*[6] But is this assumption obviously correct? Suppose that if you were to divert the trolley, you would do it with the bad intention of killing the man on the side track. Must the proponents of the DDE say that in that case you ought not to divert the trolley at all?

It seems to me that the proponents of the DDE should not say this. If it is only because of your utter wickedness that you are such that if you diverted the trolley, you would do it with this bad intention, then the proponents of the DDE should *deny* that this entails that you ought not to divert the trolley. After all, you *ought not* to be such that, were you to divert the trolley, you would do it with this bad intention; you ought to be such that, were you to divert the trolley, you would do it with a permissible intention. So it could even be true that you *ought* to divert the trolley – although of course you should only divert the trolley with the good intention of saving the five on the main track (not with bad intention of killing the one person on the side track). In general, proponents of the DDE can happily accept that the fact that an agent is such that, if he were to do a certain thin act-type, he would do it with a bad intention does not entail that it is impermissible for the agent

---

[6] Judith Thomson (1991, 293) seems to make this assumption, since she claims that the DDE entails that a would-be bomber would have to 'decide whether he may drop the bombs by looking inward for the intention with which he would be dropping them if he dropped them'. As I explain here, I believe that it is quite mistaken to interpret the DDE as committed to this.

to do the thin act-type; indeed, this fact does not even entail that it is not true that the agent *ought* to do the thin act-type.

Instead, it seems to me, the natural way to extend the DDE from thick act-types to thin act-types is by invoking the following two principles. First, a thin act-type is *permissible* if and only if there is *some* permissible thick act-type of which that thin act-type is a part. Secondly, a thin act-type is *impermissible* if and only if *every* available thick act-type of which that thin act-type is a part is impermissible. If diverting the trolley is part of a permissible thick act-type (such as diverting the trolley in order to save the five people on the main track), it follows that it is permissible to divert the trolley – although if there is a danger that the agent will divert the trolley with a bad intention, it may be misleading just to assert that he may divert the trolley, without adding that he may only divert the trolley with this permissible intention, not with the bad intention of killing the person on the side track.

This, then, is the version of the DDE that I shall defend here. In the next section, I shall touch briefly on the question of why we should think that anything like this version of the DDE is true.

2. The DDE is sometimes viewed as if it is accepted only by a few Catholic moral theologians, who have been influenced by Thomas Aquinas. But this view seems quite mistaken to me. The fundamental idea behind the DDE is deeply engrained in a great many traditions of serious moral thinking – including legal and philosophical thinking, as well as religious thinking. Thus, for example, in the law, this idea reappears as the distinction between (i) a 'direct' or 'purposeful' intention, and (ii) an 'oblique intention' (as is often confusingly called), which consists simply of the effects that the agent *knew* the act to be likely to produce. This distinction is relevant to the law in two main ways. First, there are several criminal offences that essentially involve a direct or purposeful intention (as opposed to a mere oblique intention); for example, this distinction plays a fundamental role in the laws regarding the conduct of military personnel in warfare. Secondly, even with criminal offences that do not require a direct intention, such a direct intention will normally count as an aggravating circumstance, increasing the gravity of the offence.[7]

---

[7] The literature on this topic within legal scholarship is vast. See, for example, Douglas Husak (2009).

So I believe that the DDE is presupposed by a large number of moral beliefs that have been accepted by a large and diverse collection of moral thinkers, over a long period of time. Our default assumption should be that any idea that has been presupposed by a wide moral range of moral beliefs that have been comparatively stable over time and across cultures is likely to contain some truth buried inside it somewhere.

There is also another reason that many people have for accepting this doctrine – although unfortunately I shall not be able to set out this reason in detail here. Many of us have clear intuitions about a certain range of cases, and the DDE seems to provide the best explanation of these intuitions. Some of the philosophers who reject the DDE – such as Scanlon (2009) – have tried to provide alternative explanations for our intuitions about these cases, while philosophers who support the DDE – such as McMahan (2009) – have tried to cast doubt on these alternative explanations. In this way, these cases have already been extensively discussed by a large number of other philosophers. To save time, I shall avoid getting into this dispute here (although it does seem to me that the defenders of the DDE have had stronger arguments). Instead, I shall make a quick suggestion about what might explain *why* the DDE is true.

One notable explanation of the DDE is that of Thomas Nagel (1986, 181). According to Nagel, what is especially bad about executing an intention to bring about a bad state of affairs is that in such cases, your 'will' is being 'guided by evil'.[8] My explanation of the DDE is broadly similar to Nagel's, except that I see the DDE as ultimately just an instance of a larger phenomenon.

According to my explanation, whenever the consequences of an act include a bad state of affairs, this grounds a reason against the action; but the strength of the reason does not depend purely on the badness of this state of affairs, but also on what I have called the agent's 'degree of agential involvement' in bringing about this state of affairs. Broadly speaking, I suggest that there are two dimensions along which one can be to a greater or lesser degree 'agentially involved' in bringing about a state of affairs: the first dimension is *causal*; the second dimension is *intentional*. Along the

---

[8] Of course, it may be that your will is not *wholly* 'guided by evil', since even if your intended means are bad, your ultimate end may be good, and not bad at all. Still, your will is guided by the *whole* of your intention – including your intention to use the bad means, as well as by your intention to achieve the good end. So your will is at least *partially* guided by evil in these cases.

causal dimension, there is a crucial difference between *actively causing* a state of affairs and merely *failing to prevent* that state of affairs (in effect, this is what many philosophers think of as the distinction between *doing* and *allowing*). If you merely *fail to prevent* a state of affairs from coming about, then your degree of agential involvement in bringing about that state of affairs is much less than if you *actively cause* that state of affairs to come about.

In addition to this causal dimension of agential involvement, there is also the *intentional* dimension. Other things equal, your degree of agential involvement in bringing about a state of affairs is greater if you directly *intend* that state of affairs than if you do *not* intend that state of affairs – even if you foresaw that your act was likely to result in that state of affairs. Your agency is more involved with a consequence of your act that you intended than with a consequence that you did not intend.

When your act has a bad consequence, the more agentially involved you are in bringing about that consequence, the stronger the reason against the act will be.[9] The bad consequence is more intimately connected to the act, and so the badness of the conse-quence is more strongly reflected in the reason against the act. In general, the strength of the reason against the act seems to cor-respond to the weighted sum of the degrees of badness of each of the act's consequences – where the degree of badness of each consequence is weighted by the degree of agential involvement that the agent has in that consequence.

This then is my explanation of why the DDE is true. According to this explanation, the DDE flows from a completely general feature of reasons for action: namely, in the significance for reasons for action of the agent's degree of agential involvement in the consequences of the act. So the DDE is not just a widely-accepted idea that is supported by a wide range of intuitions; it can also be explained as flowing from a pervasive and fundamen-tal feature of the normative domain.

3. Finally, I should like to address what has come to be known as the 'closeness problem'.[10] For example, consider one of the cases

---

[9] Similarly, I believe, if your act has a *good* consequence, the more agentially involved you are in bringing about that consequence, the stronger the reason *in favour* of that act will be. For more discussion of this idea of 'agential involvement', see Wedgwood (2009).
[10] For discussions of the 'closeness problem', see Hart (1968), Quinn (1989), Bennett (1995, Chap. 11), and Predelli (2004).

of Judith Thomson (1985). A runaway trolley is hurtling towards five people who are trapped on the railway track. In this case there is no side track. Instead, a large man carrying a heavy back-pack is standing on a footbridge that crosses the railway line, and if you push the man off the bridge, the trolley will collide with him and grind to a halt before it can hit the five. Many advocates of the DDE assumed that one reason why pushing the man off the bridge is objectionable is because in so doing you intend his death.

On further reflection, however, it seems that if you push the man off the bridge, you could legitimately claim *not* to intend the man's death. You only intend that he should *collide* with the trolley, so that the collision will bring the trolley to a halt. If by some miracle he survived the collision, your intentions would not require your doing anything else to ensure that he dies; indeed, it would be entirely compatible with your intentions if you also did everything possible to maximize the chances that he survives the collision. Some proponents of the DDE have responded to this point by making the following move: they have suggested that the man's collision with the trolley is sufficiently 'close' to the man's death that we can legitimately 'redescribe' your intending the collision as tantamount to your intending his death.[11]

It seems to me, however, that this is a fatal move for proponents of the DDE to make. If the content of the intentions with which an agent is acting is not an objective psychological truth about the agent, then it is radically unclear how intentions could have the ethical significance that the DDE takes them to have. But if it is an objective psychological truth what the contents of your intentions are, then we cannot simply 'redescribe' your intentions in whatever way seems convenient to us.

As we have seen, the intention with which you act is a thought that in the relevant way *guides* or *regulates* your behaviour in acting. When you push the man off the bridge, the thought that is guiding you is 'Let's make sure that he collides with the trolley' – not 'Let's make sure that he gets killed'. For these reasons, the proponents of the DDE must accept that in the bridge case, you intend the collision but *not* the death.

<hr/>

[11] Alison MacIntyre (2001) assumes that proponents of the DDE will have to use the notion of an 'intention' in this way. Fortunately for me, most of MacIntyre's criticisms do not apply to versions of the DDE that follow my recommendation and avoid using the notion of an 'intention' in this way.

Fortunately, this is no problem for my version of the DDE, since my version is not restricted to cases of intending *death*, but applies to all cases where one intends a *bad state of affairs*. So long as the collision counts as a relevantly 'bad state of affairs', intending the collision will be in my sense a bad intention, and my version of the DDE will still apply to this case. Indeed, it seems that your intention would be even *worse* if you intended not just the collision but the death as well; this seems to be because in the relevant sense the death is itself a *worse* state of affairs than the collision.

So to solve the closeness problem, we need to find a conception of a 'bad state of affairs' according to which the man's colliding with the trolley is a bad state of affairs, but the man's death is an even worse state of affairs.

It might seem obvious: surely the collision is a bad state of affairs simply because it causes the man to suffer harm? But it is equally true that the trolley's being diverted onto the side track in the original trolley case causes harm to the person on the side track. If the trolley's being diverted onto the side track counts as a relevantly 'bad state of affairs', then intending to divert the trolley onto the side track will also be a bad intention, and so the DDE will apply to the original trolley case as well.

In short, to solve this problem we need a conception of 'bad states of affairs' that has the following implications: the man's death and the man's colliding with the trolley are both bad states of affairs, although the death is a worse state of affairs than the collision; and the trolley's being diverted onto the side track is not in the relevant sense a bad state of affairs at all.

It is clear that the man's colliding with the trolley is not an *intrinsically* bad state of affairs. It is bad only because of certain additional attendant circumstances (for example, it would not be bad if the man were completely invulnerable to any injuries that the collision might cause). But in fact, the man's death is also not intrinsically bad either. The man's death will certainly be a bad state of affairs if the man has a good life and wishes to go on living. But if he is suffering from an excruciating degenerative disease and longs for death, then his death is arguably not a bad state of affairs. So the man's death is also not intrinsically bad: it is bad only because of certain additional attendant circumstances (such as the fact that the man wishes to go on living, or that his death deprives him of a reasonably good life, or the like).

As I am thinking of intrinsic value, a state of affairs has a certain degree of intrinsic value if and only if it is metaphysically necessary that that state of affairs must have that degree of intrinsic value in any possible world in which it exists. It follows that the only states of affairs that have intrinsic value are tremendously *detailed* states of affairs: each such state of affairs includes within itself everything that is relevant to determining the degree of intrinsic goodness or badness that it has.[12] It is only such highly detailed states of affairs that are, as Zimmerman (2001, 142) would put it, 'evaluatively adequate'.

The states of affairs that we *intend* are almost never such highly detailed states of affairs. Even if a murderer intends his victim's death, he will typically not intend in addition that his victim should be deprived of a life that is worth living. Since we are looking for a kind of 'badness' that is exemplified by the states of affairs that the agent *intends*, it seems that it will have to be some sort of *extrinsic* badness.

Here is a proposal about what the relevant sort of extrinsic badness is. Suppose that you are a reasonably virtuous person, and you hear the news that someone has collided with a runaway trolley. You would presumably respond by thinking, 'Oh no, how awful! That sounds terrible!' Now suppose that you hear the news that a runaway railway trolley was diverted onto a side track. You would naturally respond by thinking, 'So what? That doesn't sound very interesting.' In short, a person's colliding with a fast-moving railway trolley is in some way *bad news*, while a trolley's being diverted onto a side track is not bad news in the same way.

When you take the person's colliding with the trolley to be bad news, it seems that you would somehow be being guided by your knowledge of a range of *ceteris paribus* moral generalizations – such as, for example, the generalization that other things equal, and under normal conditions, when a collision between a person and a runaway railway trolley occurs, the person suffers serious injury or even death as a result. In general, to be a virtuous agent, it is not enough just to know the pure moral truths (of the sort that might form the fundamental principles of an abstract moral theory); it is also crucial to know a range of true *ceteris paribus* moral generalizations of this sort. A virtuous agent will form *expectations* on the basis of these *ceteris paribus* generalizations; it is these

---

[12] For more discussion of this aspect of intrinsic value, see Wedgwood (2009) and Zimmerman (2001).

expectations that the virtuous agent will express by greeting some pieces of information as good news, and others as bad news.[13]

Roughly, then, I propose that for a state of affairs S to count as a bad state of affairs in the relevant way is for the following two conditions to be met: first, a virtuous agent, guided by her knowledge of these true *ceteris paribus* moral generalizations, would form the kind of expectations about S that would lead her to view it as bad news in this way; and secondly, in this particular case, these expectations are borne out – that is, things turn out badly in more or less the very way in which S would lead such a virtuous agent to expect them to.

This is clearly a kind of extrinsic badness, since the badness of a state of affairs can vary from possible world to possible world as the true *ceteris paribus* generalizations also vary from world to world. Nonetheless, it is still a kind of *agent-neutral* badness: all virtuous agents will view the state of affairs as bad news in the same way, regardless of their particular relationships to the individual people or objects that are involved in that state of affairs.

Whenever S counts as a bad state of affairs of this kind, and an agent intends this state of affairs S, this intention counts as a 'bad intention' in my sense. By intending this state of affairs S, the agent's will is being 'guided' by a certain kind of 'evil' – that is, by what virtuous agents would regard as bad news; in this way, in effect, the agent's will is swimming against the normative tide that is created by these *ceteris paribus* generalizations.

According to my proposed interpretation of the DDE, then, when an agent successfully executes a bad intention of this sort, there is a stronger reason against the act than there would have been against an otherwise similar act that is not done with such a bad intention.

Let us examine how this solution to the closeness problem will deal with some problem cases, starting with a case that was first discussed by Foot (1978). Suppose that you blow up a man who is trapped in the mouth of a cave, so that you and your friends can

---

[13] If pushing the man off the bridge is rational, it is presumably done with the intention of solving a certain practical problem – the problem of how to save the five from the runaway trolley. This problem only exists because the trolley is moving sufficiently fast to pose a lethal risk to the five. So it seems to me that in pushing the man off the bridge, you are acting with the intention of ensuring that he collides with (and so halts) a trolley that is moving at that sort of life-threatening speed. It is surely especially clear this intended state of affairs is a bad state of affairs in this sense.

escape from the cave before being drowned by the rising tide. In this case, you intend that the man should be blown to pieces, but not that he should die: the thought that is guiding your behaviour is 'Let's ensure that he is blown to pieces' – not 'Let's make sure that he ends up dead'. Still, his being blown to pieces is a bad state of affairs in the relevant way, and so the intention with which you act is still a bad intention.

Now consider the following case, which is due to Stefano Predelli (2004). Suppose that the Reds are at war with the Blues, and the Red military command wishes to induce the Blue government to surrender immediately, by making them believe that the entire population of the Blues' second-largest city has been annihilated. All communications between the Blue capital and the Blues' second city have been severed by bombing, and so the only way for the Reds to convince the Blue government that the second city has been annihilated is by detonating bombs in the air above the city where they can be seen from the hills around the Blue capital. Unfortunately, detonating these bombs will have the foreseen but unintended effect of annihilating the city. In this case, the detonation of the bombs is intended, but the annihilation of the city is not. Nonetheless the detonation of the bombs is surely still bad news in the relevant way. So intending the detonation of the bombs is a bad intention in my sense.

Now, let us consider some cases to which my interpretation of the DDE does not apply. First, suppose that I intend to catch your attention, so that you will look up and notice that I am in the room, because this is the agreed signal that will alert a spy who is observing us, thereby enabling the spy to defuse a bomb that would otherwise kill many people. (Suppose that I know that there is no other way in which the bomb can be defused if I do not catch your attention in this way.) I have also just found out that you have a bizarre condition so that when I catch your attention in this way, it will result in your instant death.

In this case, my intention is not a bad intention: there is no true *ceteris paribus* moral generalization to the effect that under normal conditions, catching a person's attention results in any serious injury or harm. So my interpretation of the DDE does not apply here: there is presumably a reason against the act grounded in the fact that the act will kill you, but there is no reason (of the kind distinctive of the DDE) grounded in the fact that this act is the execution of a bad intention. In this case, Warren Quinn's (1989) version of the DDE yields a different verdict: in this case, I do intend to involve you in my actions in a certain way, at the same time as knowing that your being involved in that way will harm you – and that is enough for the case to involve Quinn's interpretation of the DDE. It seems to me that my verdict on the case is more plausible than Quinn's.

Finally, suppose that a judge intends to send a convicted offender to prison. Admittedly, there *is* a true *ceteris paribus* generalization to the effect that, other things equal, when an offender is imprisoned, the offender's family suffers. But there are also other true *ceteris paribus* generalizations here as well – when a convicted offender is imprisoned, the offender's victims receive justice, other criminals are deterred from committing crimes, and so on. On balance, then, a virtuous agent would not react to the news that a convicted criminal has been imprisoned by thinking 'Oh no! That sounds terrible!' So the intention to send the offender to prison is not obviously a bad intention in the relevant way.

I suggested above that an intention to bring about a man's death would typically be *worse* than an intention to bring it about that the man collides with the trolley. Presumably, this is because the man's death is in the relevant way a worse state of affairs than the collision. In general, if one state of affairs S_1 is in the relevant way *worse* than a second state of affairs S_2, then an intention to bring about S_1 will typically be a worse intention than an intention to bring about S_2.

How are we to make sense of the relevant notion of 'worse' states of affairs? The *ceteris paribus* moral generalizations that I referred to above are in effect generalizations over possible cases. This suggests that it may be possible, at least in principle, to develop a *measure* on this space of possibilities – a measure that would presumably have the structure of a *probability function.* (Intuitively, this probability function would correspond to the degrees of belief that ideally rational agents would have if their knowledge consisted *solely* of all and only these true *ceteris paribus* moral generalizations, and did not include any knowledge about the particular case at hand.) Then we can use this probability function to define the *expected badness* of a state of affairs.

Specifically, this is what I have in mind. Let P_{cp} be the probability function that corresponds to these *ceteris paribus* moral generalizations in the way that I have described. If S is a state of affairs, and W is a possible world, let $IV(W)$ be the degree of intrinsic value of W. Then we can say that if S is in the sense that I have just defined a bad state of affairs, its precise degree of badness is the conditionally expected value of $IV(W)$ on the assumption of S, according to the probability function P_{CP} – that is,

In other words, S's degree of badness is the weighted sum of the degrees of intrinsic value of each relevant possible world W, weighted by the conditional probability (according to this probability function P_{CP}) of W on the condition that S occurs.

This conception of a state of affairs' degree of badness can explain why the man's death is a worse state of affairs than the collision between the man and the trolley. Although the man's collision with the trolley is bad news, the man's death is even worse news: not all collisions result in death, and so the man's death has an even greater expectation of harm than the collision. For this reason, intending the death is an even worse intention than merely intending the collision.

We can put this point in terms of the notion of 'agential involvement' that I introduced in Section 2. If your act has an intrinsically bad consequence – like the man's losing a life worth living through being killed by the collision with the trolley – and you intend some state of affairs that is part of that consequence, then the worse this intention is (in the sense that I have just defined), the greater your degree of agential involvement in this bad consequence, and the stronger the reason against the act.

In this way, it seems possible to defend a version of the DDE against the closeness problem. In general, I hope to have made it plausible here that the DDE has the resources to rebut many of the criticisms that have been raised against it.[14]

References

Bennett, Jonathan (1995). *The Act Itself* (Oxford: Clarendon Press).

Bratman, Michael E. (1987). *Intentions, Plans, and Practical Reason* (Cambridge, Massachusetts: Harvard University Press).

[14] I am grateful to audiences at the University of Toronto, Trinity College Dublin, the Australian National University, and a conference held in memory of Philippa Foot at Somerville College, Oxford, and to several Oxford colleagues of mine, for helpful comments. I wrote this paper during my tenure of a Research Fellowship from the Leverhulme Trust, to whom I also express my gratitude.

Foot, Philippa (1978). 'The Problem of Abortion and the Doctrine of the Double Effect', reprinted in Foot, *Virtues and Vices* (Oxford: Blackwell).

Goldman, Alvin (1970). *A Theory of Human Action* (Englewood Cliffs, New Jersey: Prentice-Hall).

Hart, H. L. A. (1968). 'Intention and Punishment', reprinted in Hart, *Punishment and Responsibility* (Oxford: Oxford University Press).

Husak, Douglas (2009). 'The Costs to Criminal Theory of Supposing that Intentions are Irrelevant to Permissibility', *Criminal Law and Philosophy* 3: 51–70.

Jackson, Frank and Pargetter, Robert (1986). 'Oughts, Options, and Actualism', *Philosophical Review* 95: 233–55.

Lewis, David (1973). *Counterfactuals* (Oxford: Blackwell).

MacIntyre, Alison (2001). 'Doing Away with *Double Effect*', *Ethics*, 111(2): 219–255.

McMahan, Jeff (2009). 'Intention, Permissibility, Terrorism, and War', *Philosophical Perspectives* 23: 345–72.

Mele, Al (2000). 'Goal-Directed Action: Teleological Explanations, Causal Theories, And Deviance', *Philosophical Perspectives* 14: 279–300.

Nagel, Thomas (1986). *The View from Nowhere* (Oxford: Clarendon Press).

Predelli, Stefano (2004). 'Bombers: Some Comments on Double Effect and Harmful Involvement', *Journal of Military Ethics* 3: 16–26.

Quinn, Warren (1989). 'Actions, Intentions, and Consequences: The Doctrine of Double Effect', *Philosophy & Public Affairs* 18(1989): 334–351.

Scanlon, T. M. (2009). *Moral Dimensions: Permissibility, Meaning, Blame* (Cambridge, Massachusetts: Harvard University Press).

Thomson, Judith (1985). 'The Trolley Problem', *Yale Law Journal* 94: 1395–1415.

—— (1991). 'Self-Defense', *Philosophy and Public Affairs* 20: 283–310.

—— (1999). 'Physician-Assisted Suicide: Two Moral Arguments', *Ethics* 109: 497–518.

Wedgwood, Ralph (2009). 'Intrinsic Values and Reasons for Action', *Philosophical Issues* 19: 342–363.

—— (2011). 'Scanlon on Double Effect', *Philosophy and Phenomenological Research*, forthcoming.

Zimmerman, Michael J. (2001). *The Nature of Intrinsic Value* (Lanham, Maryland: Rowman & Littlefield).

4

THE POSSIBILITY OF CONSENT

David Owens

Abstract

Worries about the possibility of consent recall a more familiar problem about promising raised by Hume. To see the parallel here we must distinguish the *power of consent* from the *normative significance of choice*. I'll argue that we have normative interests, interests in being able to control the rights and obligations of ourselves and those around us, interests distinct from our interest in controlling the non-normative situation. Choice gets its normative significance from our non-normative control interests. By contrast, the possibility of consent depends on a species of normative interest that I'll call a permissive interest, an interest in its being the case that certain acts wrong us unless we declare otherwise. In the final section, I'll show how our permissive interests underwrite the possibility of consent.

1. The Problem of Normative Power

On the face of it, we can often change the normative situation simply by communicating the intention of hereby changing the normative situation. For example, I can put myself under an obligation to meet you at 4 pm by promising to meet you at 4 pm. To promise you this is just to communicate to you the intention of putting myself under this obligation to you by means of this very communication, namely the communication of an intention to put myself under this obligation. In promising, one alters one's obligations by *declaration*.[1] Now promising is not the only way of altering the normative situation by declaration: giving, commanding and indeed consenting all affect what obligations people have by means of an essentially similar mechanism. I shall say that promising, giving, commanding and consenting are all forms of *normative power*, by which I mean that they are all powers to change the normative situation by declaration.

---

[1] This claim is familiar but not uncontroversial. I defend it in *Shaping the Normative Landscape* (Oxford: Oxford University Press, forthcoming).

Developing Deontology, First Edition. Edited by Brad Hooker. Copyright © 2012 The Authors. Book compilation © 2012 Blackwell Publishing Ltd.

Hume famously doubted the intelligibility of promising understood as the exercise of normative power. Speaking of promising in the *Treatise*, he says:

> 'tis one of the most mysterious and incomprehensible operations that can possibly be imagined, and may even be compared to *transubstantiation*, or *holy orders*, where a certain form of words, along with a certain intention, changes entirely the nature of an external object, and even of a human creature[2]

What is worrying Hume? Here is a first stab: to be obliged to do something is at least to have a serious reason to do it. Prior to my promise, I have no reason to meet you at 4 pm. If my promise binds me then it must create such a reason *ex nihilo*. But how can I create a serious reason to do something simply by declaring that I am hereby creating such a reason? To put it another way, how can it make some sense for me to keep this promise simply because I have declared that it does make some sense?

This diagnosis is along the right lines but more needs to be said about exactly why Hume doubts that mere declarations are a source of reasons for action. Hume (and many others) assume that reasons (or at least motives) for action have their source in facts about what is good for human beings, facts about what is in their interests. This is not egoism: other people's interests can move me to action. Nor is it facile optimism: we frequently choose the lesser good over the greater. Hume simply doubts that people can sensibly aim at what will bring nobody any good. Given this Humean assumption, the problem is clear: I can't change how my meeting you at 4 pm will affect anyone's interests simply by declaration. Therefore my declaration cannot be a source of reasons for action.

Scrutiny of Hume's examples confirms the correctness of this diagnosis. For instance,

> I suppose a person to have lent me a sum of money, on condition that it be restored in a few days; and also suppose that, after the expiration of the term agreed on, he demands the sum: I ask, *what reason or motive have I to restore the money?*[3]

---

[2] David Hume, *Treatise on Human Nature* (Oxford: Oxford University Press, 1978), p. 524.

[3] Hume, *Treatise*, p. 479.

For what if he be my enemy, and has given me just cause to hate him? What if he be a vicious man, and deserves the hatred of all mankind? What if he be a miser, and can make no use of what I would deprive him of? What if he be a profligate debauchee, and would rather receive harm than benefit from large possessions? What if I be in necessity, and have urgent motives to acquire something to my family? In all these cases, the original motive to justice would fail; and consequently the justice itself, and along with it all property, right and obligation.[4]

In this case, it would do nobody any good and some people (including the promisee) a great deal of harm for Hume to keep his promise. Yet few moralists would allow that these facts alone extinguish Hume's obligation to return the money.[5] Whatever Hume ought to do all things considered, they suppose that he has a serious reason to return the money.

I'll call breach of a valid promise which involves no action against any human interests a *bare wronging*. Normative powers are devices for manufacturing bare wrongings and Hume's doubts about the intelligibility of normative power stem from his doubts about the status of bare wrongings. In the first of the above quotations, Hume asserts the impossibility of changing 'the nature of an external object, and even of a human creature' by a mere 'form of words'. Here he is assuming that we can render some deed worthy of avoidance only by changing the non-normative situation in such a way that the occurrence of that deed would adversely affect some human interest. And we surely can't make such changes simply by declaring that something is wrongful. Therefore we can't make the deed any more worthy of avoidance simply by declaring it to be wrongful.

Two queries should be dealt with before moving on. First, it may be objected that the wrong of breach of promise is never created *simply* by declaration. All sorts of conditions need to be satisfied for a promise to bind: the declaration must have been made by a competent party, not acting under duress nor the victim of a trick, the action promised must be feasible and perhaps also morally permissible. Further conditions might be added but none of this resolves Hume's difficulty. Each of these conditions

4 Hume, *Treatise*, p. 482.
5 Hume, *Treatise*, pp. 480–81.

may be satisfied without ensuring that breach of promise is anything other than a bare wrong and this is so because mere declaration plays a crucial role in creating that wrong.

Second, is Hume's problem symptomatic of the philosopher's obsession with marginal cases? Very few actual breaches of promise constitute bare wrongings. For one thing, promisees tend to expect promises to be kept and tend to act in reliance on them or at least feel disappointment when they are breached. For another, promisees tend to extract promises only when they have some interest in their fulfilment and this interest may be harmed whether or not they trust the promisor to keep their word. Finally, though we do put some weight on promises whose fulfilment will do nobody any good, they are hardly the promises we take most seriously. Why construct our account of promising around such an atypical instance of the breed?

If promising really does involve an exercise of normative power then this objection is misguided. Here we must distinguish the primary wrong of breach of promise from the secondary wrongs which often accompany it. True, promisees usually expect promisors to keep their promise. Why so? The most obvious answer is that they expect them to keep their promise because they think them obliged to keep it. So the secondary wrong of disappointing the promisee's expectations exists only because there is thought to be a prior wrong of breach of promise. Furthermore, the harm to the promisee's interests that often results from breach of promise may constitute a wrong to the promisee only because they received an assurance that it would not occur: the harm's status as a secondary wronging depends on the breach's status as a primary wrong. So if we want to understand what is really going on in the typical case of breach where the primary wrong generates various secondary wrongs, we would do well to focus on the marginal case to which Hume directs our attention, the case in which the primary wrong stands alone.

Now let's turn to consent. Both promise and consent determine who is wronged by a certain act but whilst promising creates an obligation, consent abolishes it. A promise ensures that the promisee is wronged by a breach that might otherwise be innocuous; consent ensures that the consentor is not wronged by some deed that would otherwise be far from innocuous. For Hume, the problem of normative power was raised as much by the phenomenon of consent as by the practice of promising (and a similar solution was required):

Were the interests of society nowise concerned, it is as unintelligible, why another's articulating certain sounds, implying
consent, should change the nature of my actions with regard to
a particular object, as why the reciting of a liturgy by a priest, in
a certain habit and posture, should dedicate a heap of brick
and timber, and render it, thenceforth and forever, sacred.[6]

It is clear enough what Hume has in mind. If I invite you into my
home, at least part of what I am doing is to *permit* you to enter, is
to declare that you would not wrong me by entering. And such a
declaration can make all the difference between an innocuous
entry and a trespass. But how? How can I make it the case that you
wouldn't wrong me simply by communicating the intention of
hereby ensuring that you would not wrong me? If there is a serious
reason for you not to enter my house, how can I abolish that
reason by declaration?

In the case of promising, I traced Hume's doubts about the
possibility of normative power to his doubts about the existence of
bare wrongings. The example of trespass fits that diagnosis nicely.
It is not hard to imagine cases of trespass which constitute bare
wrongings and even where trespass causes harm of some sort, we
may well be able to argue, as we did in the case of promising, that
such harms are by-products of the bare wrong of trespass.[7] It is
much less obvious that our diagnosis can cope with consent to sex
or to a medical procedure. Are the wrongs, the violations of bodily
integrity that would occur in the absence of consent, really bare
wrongings?

I shall argue that the wrongs rendered innocuous by consent
are all bare wrongings, are all wrongings which affect no human
interest. And once their status as bare wrongings is acknowledged,
there is no mystery about how mere declaration could affect their
status as wrongings. It is perfectly intelligible to suppose that bare
wrongings are created and abolished by declaration. To see how
that might all be so, we must first distinguish exercises of the
power of consent from other ways in which human choice can
affect the normative situation.

---

[6]   David Hume, *Enquiry Concerning the Principles of Morals* (Oxford: Oxford University
Press, 1975), p. 208.
[7]   J. Gardner and S. Shute, 'The Wrongness of Rape', in J. Gardner (ed.), *Offences and
Defences* (Oxford: Oxford University Press, 2007), pp. 11–12.

2. Consent and Choice

The English word 'consent' and its cousins 'permit', 'authorise', 'allow' can refer to a form of promise. To consent to your driving my car tomorrow may involve agreeing to this, i.e. promising you the use of my car. (Perhaps that is how Hume is employing the term.) But I shall use 'consent' to mark a phenomenon which shares in the mystery of promising without itself being a form of promise.

On my usage, consent involves not the granting of a right but just the waiving of it. To consent to S's dentistry is to intentionally communicate the intention of hereby making it the case that S does not wrong you by whitening your teeth, etc. This intention can be communicated in any number of ways (silence *can* mean consent). On this usage, having consented to dentistry tomorrow, you may withdraw your consent. (There is no such thing as revoking a promise.) Or else, without actually withdrawing your consent, you may do things which make it impossible for S to take advantage of it: like traveling to another city. And you may do these things without yourself wronging S *simply* because you previously consented (rather than because you have aroused expectations and so forth). In consenting you undertake no obligation to ensure that others can take advantage of your consent. I don't deny that an act of consent to dental treatment often implies some sort of agreement to co-operate with the dentist. Frequently there would be little point consenting to something unless you meant to facilitate its occurrence. But, as we shall see, this is not invariably true and even when it is true, in consenting to X you might just be communicating a present intention of allowing X to happen whilst retaining the option of calling things off: 'OK go ahead but once I discover how painful the teeth-whitening actually is I might not be able to go through with it' or else 'OK you can do it provided I'm around to have it done'. Here you consent to a procedure without committing to it.[8]

Consent, like promise, raises the problem of normative power, yet the magic of consent receives much less attention than the magic of promising. I suspect that we are less troubled by the former because we tend to confuse the power of consent with a

---

[8]   Joseph Raz, *The Morality of Freedom* (Oxford: Oxford University Press, 1986), pp. 82–3.

rather different phenomenon, namely the significance of choice.[9] In ordinary talk, 'consent' is freely used where choice is what really does the work; but we must differentiate and, I propose, the best way of so doing is to reserve 'consent to X' for cases where you (intentionally) communicate the intention of hereby making it the case that someone would not wrong you by X-ing.

Before focusing on the power of consent, let's first consider the significance of choice. How might whether S wrongs you by doing X to you depend on your choices? Suppose S sticks a knife into me. If the knifing is part of a medical procedure which I have chosen rather than part of a mugging which I have not, it is unlikely to wrong me. But why? An obvious suggestion is this: choice bears on the normative status of an action where we have an interest in having the occurrence of such actions depend on our choices. On this hypothesis, the significance of choice reflects our interest in controlling what is done to us.

We may have such a control interest for quite a number of reasons. For one thing, the fact that someone has chosen to be subjected to a medical procedure may itself be a good indication that it is in their interests to be subjected to the procedure. Provided they are free to choose and well-informed, the patient may be the best judge of whether it is worth their while to suffer the pain and expense of surgery given the benefits that may be forthcoming. Similarly, the fact that someone has chosen to walk onto the football field may be the best indication that it is in their interests to participate in this contact sport with all the risks entailed. Here it is a good thing if what happens to one depends on one's choices because what happens is more likely to be in one's interests if one has chosen it. And whether X is likely to be in my interests is obviously relevant to the question of whether X wrongs me.

Furthermore, the fact that I have chosen X may actually *make* it the case that X is in my interests rather than merely indicate that this is so. People often enjoy things that they have chosen or actively decided upon over things that merely happen to them

---

[9]   The parallel between promise and consent is highlighted with a view to making promising seem less problematic by Herbert Hart, 'Are There Any Natural Rights?', *Philosophical Review* 64 (1955), p. 184; Judith Thomson, *The Realm of Rights* (Cambridge: Harvard University Press, 1995), pp. 350–51; Seana Shiffrin, 'Promising, Intimate Relationships and Conventionalism', *Philosophical Review* 117 (2008), pp. 500–01 and Gary Watson, 'Promises, Reasons and Normative Powers', in D. Sobel and S. Wall (eds), *Reasons for Action* (Cambridge: Cambridge University Press, 2009), section 4.

regardless of their choice. They enjoy choosing to enact something worthwhile like a football match. Here the enjoyability of
the chosen activity enhances its value. One might have enjoyed
the football match even if one had been forced to take part but
such enjoyment would have a lesser (or at least a different kind
of) value. Additionally (or alternatively), my voluntary participation in the match may be a good both for me and for others
because it expresses my adherence to a certain valuable sporting
tradition and my participation has this expressive significance
only because it depends on my choice. In both of these ways, the
fact that I have chosen to walk onto the football field may help to
make it the case that others do not wrong me when they crush and
tackle me.[10]

Choice often carries a further social meaning. For example,
much of human life is governed by considerations of honor.
Certain deeds attract admiration and bestow prestige whilst others
humiliate or embarrass. Clearly it is in our interests to be admired
because of rather than to be embarrassed by what happens to us
and whether our interactions with others are a source of prestige
or shame is frequently a function of whether we chose them. Take
bodily exposure. Often it is not embarrassing to be observed
naked or to be seen dressed as a fairy provided one has chosen to
be so observed. One does not incur the same disdain when one's
appearance is obviously deliberate (acting, working as a model,
swimming, etc.) and where this is so, it is in our interests to be able
to choose whether we are exposed to public view. Other forms of
social meaning are comparative. If I live in a society in which most
people are allowed the choice of whether to wear a crash helmet
whilst cycling, the fact that I (and people like me) are deprived of
this choice will be demeaning. It carries the message that they are
competent to decide this matter but I am not.[11] And this may be so
whether or not choice has, in this instance, the other forms of
social and psychological significance just described. Given that I
have an interest in not being demeaned, I also have an interest in
having the ability to control my headwear.

I conclude that choice bears on the normative status of an
action where we have an interest in controlling such actions by
means of our choices. It is worth noting that this control interest

---

[10]   Thomas Scanlon, *What We Owe to Each Other* (Cambridge MA.: Harvard University
Press 1998), pp. 251–53; Raz, *Morality of Freedom*, pp. 84–88.
[11]   Scanlon, *What We Owe*, p. 253.

is in play even when there is no question of anyone's being harmed. Though many acts are wrongs because they harm someone's interests, some are wrongs for a rather different reason, namely because they are unfair, an unfairness which need not involve harm, e.g. where you get an unfair share of the proceeds of our co-operative enterprise. Here the rest of us might both benefit from and deserve to get a larger share of the products of our joint enterprise, even if being 'deprived' of this share constitutes no *harm* to us. Now just as citing the victim's choice is a defence against the allegation that you wronged them by harming them, so choice can rebut the allegation that your behaviour was unfair to us. For example if we, your partners in the co-operative enterprise, freely choose to grant you such generous terms, this may well remove the unfairness. Our choice has normative significance here because our interest in the distribution of these benefits gives us an interest in controlling how they are distributed for the reasons already canvassed.

Having reviewed some of the ways in which having a choice can matter to us, we are now in a position to see how choice, operating independently of consent, can influence the normative situation. Recall that to consent to S's X-ing was to intentionally communicate the intention of hereby ensuring that S does not wrong you by X-ing. Choice does its normative work rather differently. First, choice in the above examples has a non-normative object. The patient chooses to undergo surgery, the football player chooses to take the risk of being hit, etc. Their choices may ensure that certain physical assaults no longer wrong them but what they are choosing is the surgery and the risk, not the normative status of the assault. Second, it is the choice and not the communication of the choice which matters. If my choice makes it OK for the surgeon and the other players to touch me then provided they know of my choice, they are not blameworthy for so doing. It does not matter whether they learnt this fact because I intentionally let them know that this was my choice.

This last point is particularly obvious where your action has its impact on me even though there is no further interaction between us. Do you wrong me by possessing some offensive drawings? That might depend on whether you put them in a place where I am likely to see them without choosing to. If I see them only because I chose to see them then my objection to being shocked is undermined and this has nothing to do with whether I have communicated my choice to you or anyone else, intentionally or otherwise. Nor does it depend on my views about how my choice will affect the normative situation: perhaps I will feel wronged by the sight of your drawings regardless. What gets you off the hook (with regards to my shock) is simply that you knew I would see them only if I chose to.

Despite these differences it is no surprise that the significance of choice and the power of consent are often equated. My sitting in the dentist's chair, or walking onto the football field, does have the effect of letting others know that I have made a certain choice. Furthermore I typically know that fact. Therefore it is usually the case that I intentionally communicate my choice by so acting. Finally, I typically know that my choice will have a certain effect on the normative situation. Therefore, it is usually the case that when I make a normatively significant choice I intentionally change the normative situation. Nonetheless the normative significance of my choice here need not depend on any of this. It might depend only on its being known that I have chosen (or am very likely to have chosen) the surgery or the game.

Consent needs to be communicated to be valid. It is noteworthy that the same is true of other exercises of normative powers such as promising and commanding. You are not wronging me by failing to show up at 4 pm unless you have communicated to me the intention of *hereby* (i.e. by means of this very communication) obliging yourself to appear. Perhaps you can inwardly vow to meet me at 4 pm but, even supposing such vows do bind, you do not owe it *to me* to appear. And this is so even if you happen to tell me about your vow (setting the effect on my expectations aside). Some might think that this is because a promise must be accepted by the promisee to be binding and nobody can accept a promise which hasn't been communicated to them. I agree that binding promises must be offered and accepted but I doubt this is what explains the need for communication. An order need not be accepted to be valid but it must be communicated. I can't put my subordinates under an obligation to do anything simply by performing an inner mental act. Even if they somehow learn of this act, they still haven't been told to do anything and it is the telling which binds.

3. Promise, Consent and Normative Interests

So what is the function of consent? What does this social tool do for us which can't be done by making choices? Consent enables us to determine by declaration whether something constitutes a wronging. Who would benefit from having such a power? Creatures with only non-normative control interests could get by without. Human beings are not such creatures. We need to mould our normative niche. But do we need the capacity to do so by declaration?

You are giving a lecture at a conference with parallel sessions. In the way of these things, it is likely that a significant proportion of your audience is sitting in the room under a misapprehension as to whose lecture this is. They'll discover their error once you start to speak and will likely wish to leave. But, at least in many social contexts, it is rather rude to leave a lecture once the speaker has begun. Without the ability to remove this element of rudeness, you are faced with the prospect of having to endure either the insult of a mass exodus or the restlessness of a captive audience. There is a way out. You can begin your talk by announcing your name and topic and inviting those who are here by mistake to take the opportunity to leave the room. Then (in many social contexts) they can leave without wronging you.

How should we understand this announcement of yours? One might construe it as the expression of a choice: you intend that those in the room under a misapprehension should leave. But this may not be what you intend at all. Haven't we all found ourselves in talks unwillingly and then been unexpectedly entranced by the speaker and their subject? Mightn't you imagine that the same will happen once you begin to speak? Entertaining such hopes, you do not intend that people leave just because they are there by mistake, nor are you trying to communicate such an intention. Rather your announcement is directed at the normative situation. You mean to alter the normative significance of their leaving the room should they (against your wishes) choose to do so. You mean to ensure that their departure would not be an insult by consenting to it. Thus, we have a power of consenting to X whose exercise involves no choice of X, no intention that X occur.

Our lecturer example indicates that we have an interest in controlling the normative situation by declaration. This interest in controlling the normative situation comes apart form our interest in controlling what happens in two ways. On the one hand, there are cases in which we grant a privilege without either having or communicating the intention that it be exercised. For example one can invite people to a party whom one neither wants nor expects to show up, a fact they may be well aware of. Here you give them the right to show up without either having or communicating any intention that they show up. Perhaps you invite them for form's sake and just don't care whether they show up. Perhaps you invite them in order to ensure that they won't show up (they won't come when invited by *you*, though they would have had your partner invited them first). Either way, you have granted them the right to attend.

Conversely, we sometimes communicate the intention that someone be at our party without thereby consenting to their being there, without thereby making it the case that their presence would not wrong us. Suppose I want Kate to attend but Kate has had a falling out with my partner. I tell Kate 'I'd love you to come but I prefer not to invite you myself. I would rather my partner invite you and they will do so only if you ask them'. Here I am telling Kate that I'd like her to come, without thereby consenting to her coming, even though I have an (independent) power of consent. If Kate showed up without bothering to get permission from my partner, Kate would be wronging us both since neither of us has consented.[12]

Given the many different ways in which our choices can affect the normative situation, why do we need a power of consent? Why do we need to be able to control the normative situation directly by declaration? I reckon we need consent to serve a normative interest. Once more, the parallel with promising is suggestive. A promisee can release the promisor from their promise, can consent to non-performance. For Hobbes, all obligations – indeed all wrongings – had their source in promising and so, for Hobbes, the power of consent just *was* the power of release.[13] Hobbes's assimilation of these two normative powers is no more plausible than the view of obligation which motivates it but the comparison between consent and release remains illuminating. One who proposes to substitute choice for consent may be asked to do the same with the power of release. And the difficulties which confront the project of substituting choice for release reveal the flaws in the project of substituting choice for consent.

Promising is here to serve the promisee's authority interest, an interest in having a certain form of control over the normative situation, in being able to choose whether others are required to

---

[12] I'm not consenting conditional on my partner's consenting since my consent is redundant once they have consented.

[13] Thomas Hobbes, *Leviathan* (Indianapolis: Hackett, 1994), p. 94.

fulfill a promise.[14] This authority interest can be satisfied only if the promisee has power of release. For a promise to bind it must be both offered and accepted and so the promisor and the promisee are on a par so far as the *creation* of the obligation goes; there is no asymmetry of authority here. It is only with the power of release that the desired asymmetry emerges. The promisee can abolish the obligation by declaration and this declaration is effective whether or not the promisor accepts it; the promisor has no similar power. This power of release employs the very mechanism by which the obligation is imposed, the communication of the intention to hereby change the normative situation. Merely intending to promise does not bind you even if you somehow let the promisee know of your intention. You must actually communicate the intention to bind yourself by way of this very communication. Similarly what releases is the intentional communication of the decision to hereby release and not the decision itself. To act in anticipation of release is to wrong the promisee. Indeed outrage at being pre-empted in this way might lead the promisee to abandon their intention to release.

Can we ground this power of release in the significance of choice?[15] That the power of release can be exercised without any expression of choice suggests a negative answer. I can release you from a promise whilst making it quite clear that I intend you to do what you promised to do. Indeed the release might be my means of getting you to perform, if I think you are more likely to do so 'of your own free will'. Conversely, I might decline to release you from a promise, whilst making it clear that I couldn't care less whether you actually perform. Perhaps I extracted the promise at the behest of a third party who wishes you to be held to it. This two-way independence of choice and release is a product of the independence of the interests these powers are here to serve. Choice gains its normative significance from our non-normative interest in controlling what happens around us; release gains its normative significance from our normative interest in controlling the obligations of those around us; and we can have the authority interest in controlling the obligations of those around us whilst lacking the interest in control over what actually happens.

---

[14] Owens, *Shaping the Normative*, ch. 6.

[15] Scanlon proposes to ground the need for 'consent to agreements' in the significance of choice. See Scanlon, *What We Owe*, p. 260 and Thomas Scanlon *The Difficulty of Tolerance* (Cambridge: Cambridge University Press, 2003), pp. 263–66.

Recall that promising generates bare wrongings. A promise can ensure that behaviour the promisor has no interest in controlling wrongs him. For example, Hume's creditor has no control interest in whether the money Hume owes him is returned: since there is no good in having the money, values of enjoyment, self expression, etc. do not apply. His debauchery ensures that his choices are not a good indication of his interests. His social standing is unaffected by secret theft, etc. Therefore his choices in this matter lack normative significance. But he retains the power of consent, the power to ensure that Hume would not be wronging him by failing to return the money. So that power must be grounded in something other than his interest in controlling what Hume does. It must be grounded in some normative interest of his, in this case an authority interest, an interest whose object is the right to the promised act rather than the promised act itself.

4. Permissive Interests

In this section, I'll seek to establish two points. First, that there are bare wrongings not created by a promise. Second, that we have an interest in being able to authorise these acts by declaration and that there is nothing unintelligible or paradoxical here. The latter *permissive interests* are what ground the power of consent.

The wrong of rape is a bare wronging.[16] This might sound absurd. Most rapists do their victim great physical or psychological damage. But, as in the case of breach of promise, we must carefully disentangle secondary wrongs from the primary wrong they accompany. In the case of promising, the primacy of the bare wronging comes out in two ways. First, there are cases in which the primary wrong occurs without its usual accompaniments but remains a serious matter. Second, the harms and other secondary wrongs which typically accompany the bare wrong acquire much of their normative significance from the context of bare wronging in which they occur. For example, where people rely on promises to their detriment and so suffer material damage when the promise is breached, outrage at being let down is reasonable because breach of promise is independently wrongful. For

---

[16] Gardner, 'The Wrongness of Rape', pp. 3–8.

analytical purposes, the central cases of breach of promise are the statistically peripheral ones in which no harm aggravates the primary wrong.

So it is with rape:

> It is possible, though unusual, for a rapist to do no harm. A victim may be forever oblivious to the fact that she was raped if, say, she was drugged or drunk to the point of unconsciousness when the rape was committed and the rapist wore a condom . . . Then we have a victim of rape whose life is not changed for the worse, or at all, by the rape. She does not . . . 'feel violated'. She has no feelings about the incident since she knows nothing of it.[17]

Gardner goes on to stipulate that nobody else learns anything of the rape and that the rapist dies soon afterward, so neither the victim's social standing nor other people's sense of security is affected. These stipulations notwithstanding, 'pure rape' as Gardner calls it is a grave wrong.

Where the victim discovers what has happened to them, the secondary wrongs kick in. They would be rightly outraged and probably shattered. And when the rape is experienced as it occurs, this experience is traumatising, even when no physical damage is done, precisely because it is the experience of a great wrong. It is crucial to grasp the order of explanation here: if what made rape wrong were the brute fact that it tended to have a shattering or traumatising effect on those who became aware of it, a tranquilizer could render it innocuous.

Consent to sexual relations is a paradigm case of an exercise of the power of consent. Merely by intentionally communicating the intention of hereby authorizing you to have sex with me, I ensure that you do not commit the egregious wrong of rape, whatever other wrong you may do me. But if rape is a bare wronging and if, as we saw a moment ago, choice gets no purchase on bare wrongings, this power of consent cannot be based on the significance of choice. Choice is normatively significant where we have an

---

[17] Gardner, 'The Wrongness of Rape', p. 5. I have seen reports of some doctors' being accused of drugging their patients and then abusing them whilst the patients were unconscious. To make Gardner's point, we need not suppose that such incidents have no adverse effects, only that their gravity is not proportional to the gravity of those effects. (And we need not assume a female victim.)

interest in our choices controlling what happens to us. In a case of 'pure rape', I have no such interest. Since there is no physical or psychological damage, nor risk of such we may suppose, there is no role for judgement (good or bad) as to whether the risk is worth it to me. Since I do nothing, no expressive value is at stake. Since I do not experience it, my experience is not an issue. Since nobody knows of the rape except for the rapist, there is no adverse or unwelcome reaction to be faced and fear will not spread through the land.

Of course rape and other violations of bodily integrity are usually dreaded quite independently of the damage involved. This fear is clearly a cost to those who suffer it but the normative significance of this dread is unclear. Why should '*pure* rape' be regarded as demeaning and humiliating given that the victim's other interests are quite untouched by it? Compare an actual 'pure' rape with someone who (deliberately) *only imagines* committing 'pure rape' on an acquaintance. The real and imaginary rapes are equally harmless we may suppose. The acquaintance would doubtless prefer that this not be imagined and may even fear its being imagined. But fear of imaginary rape lacks the normative significance of fear of real 'pure rape' and, one might suppose, this is because the wrong of imagining rape (if wrong it be) is much less grave than the wrong of committing it.

We've now established that (in our social world) there is at least one bare wronging not created by a promise: the wrong of rape. Consent operates on that wrong, a wrong on which choice gains no purchase. Furthermore, consent operates directly *only* on the bare wrong: one can't abolish merely by declaration those secondary wrongs which occur in the course of most rapes. I can't make it the case that I am not wronged by a serious physical injury, for instance, simply by declaring that this is so. The significance of the injury depends on its affecting my interests (including my control interests) and though my choices might influence how it affects my interests, my declarations alone will not.

Hume thought consent unintelligible because he made two assumptions. First, he assumed that all wronging must involve action against the interests of the wronged. Second, he assumed that if the wrongfulness of a wrong depends on how it affects our interests then one cannot remove the wrongfulness of a wrong merely by declaration. Hume's second assumption is sound but it does not apply to bare wrongings. In their case, why shouldn't one be able to affect the normative significance of the act by declaration since its normative significance does not depend on whether it promotes or undermines any human interest?

It will seem obvious to many that consent can have an impact on the normative significance of deeds other than bare wrongings. Furthermore, it may appear equally evident that, even in the absence of consent, choice can affect the normative significance of a bare wrong like rape. I'll deal with these queries in order.

As to the first, an expression of consent is often also an expression of choice, of an intention that the act consented to should actually occur as a result of the consent. And where this is so, the normative character of a physical injury may be transformed by the choice. Think of the difference between a lover's bite and a rapist's. Purely *qua* physical injury, they are on a par but one exacerbates the wrong of rape whilst the other may enhance the good of sex. Since for many lovers being able to control whether you are bitten is a good thing, their choice turns the bite into a good thing. By contrast, lobotomisation or (voluntary) enslavement can't be good in the same way whether chosen or not.[18] Doubtless choice makes some difference in their case but not such as to prevent these acts from wronging us. Hence consent does not appear to affect their normative character. The case of simple killing is more complex. Lying on the battlefield mortally wounded and in great pain, perhaps I can consent to being put out of my misery by a comrade. Here consent is significant as an expression of choice and if I have enough of an interest in being able to choose death in these circumstances, it may ensure that the killing does not wrong me.

Even where consent is not an expression of choice, consent may have an indirect impact on the significance of such injuries, physical and psychological. You do not want sex with me. Given the choice, you would rather not and you let me know as much. But, for any number of reasons, you might *not* want it to be the case that, should I go ahead anyway, that would make me a rapist and you a rape victim.[19] So you waive your veto, that is, you communicate the intention of hereby making it the case that should I go ahead despite your preferences, I would not be raping you. And, we may suppose, you do so freely (the simple

---

[18] They may have instrumental value but not value for their own sake.

[19] Consenting might even be a way of ensuring that no sex took place. A rapist aroused by the idea of rape would be discouraged by consent.

fact that you don't intend me to have sex with you need not entail the presence of a consent-invalidating duress). You could stop me but you prefer the easier option of exercising control over the normative situation. Here, because your consent is not an expression of your choice I might still be wronging you by persisting in the face of your reluctance. But I would not be committing the egregious wrong of rape and that fact alters the significance of any secondary wrongs in so far as their significance depends on the context in which they occur rather than on their intrinsic character as injuries. Your fear is no longer fear of rape and your distaste or disgust are not reactions to the experience of rape. The marks I leave are not lover's bites – they may well be a focus of embarrassment or even resentment – but nor are they remnants of a rape. By removing the primary wrong, your consent changes the character of these secondary wrongs.

I have said that to consent to X is to communicate the intention of hereby making it the case that X would not wrong you. This formulation must be refined in the light of the previous example. There, in consenting to sex, you don't set out to make it the case that sex with you would not wrong you. You know (and may indeed insist on the fact) that sex with you would still wrong you. Nevertheless, there is way in which sex would wrong you in the absence of consent and you intend to make it the case that sex does not wrong you in that way. There is a consideration against having sex with you which no longer applies once you have consented to it. The aim of consent is to abolish that consideration.

Turning to the second query, can sex that has been chosen constitute rape? It must be so if the interest which generates the wrong of rape is an interest in being wronged by sex unless you *declare* otherwise. And it is so. Someone chooses to be raped where they intend that the rapist have sex with them after they have explicitly refused their consent. This choice is perverse but by no means impossible and the choice may well make a difference to the character of what transpires. For one thing, it may lessen, or even in some cases abolish the wrongfulness of the secondary effects of the rape. But the primary wrong remains: to have sex in the teeth of an explicit refusal is to rape (a fact which may arouse the rapist). '"No" means No' even where the perpetrator is correct in supposing that the victim wishes them to go ahead.

I conclude that to explain the significance of 'pure rape' and of its antidote consent, we must ground the wrong of rape not in some interest supposedly compromised by the rape itself but rather in a normative interest, in an interest in its being the case that one is wronged by the rape *unless one consents to it.* This is what I call a permissive interest. And this interest is in play even though it is not under threat. Just as breach of promise need not harm the authority interest, so rape need not harm this permissive interest. Nevertheless, a regard for the normative status of these wrongings will prevent the conscientious from committing them.

Our objection to rape is just one aspect of our concern with bodily integrity. I am seriously wronged by medical procedures to which I do not consent, however beneficial and risk free they may be. I am mildly wronged when someone removes a hair from my head as a souvenir whilst I'm asleep. I may even be wronged by cannibals who desecrate my dead body. There are often secondary wrongs here, wrongs tied to risk of harm, or psychic distress or public humiliation but the primary wrong is clearly a violation of bodily integrity, a violation which is objectionable regardless of whether there is a loss of some form of bodily control which I might sensibly value.

The cluster of normative interests around the body encourages the thought that all such interests must be connected with non-normative interests, interests in control over what happens to our body. Imagine a world in which nobody has much interest in physical sexual activity – human beings have learned to reproduce and gain erotic pleasure in other ways – and yet vestigial sexual organs remain (rather like the appendix). In such a world, could 'pure rape' have anything like the significance it has in our own lives? And doesn't that indicate that the weighty permissive interests we have with respect to sex are embedded in those weighty non-normative interests that surround sexual activity as presently constituted?

Perhaps our normative interests such as our permissive interests are not independent of our non-normative interests. Still various modes of connection would preserve the distinctness and irreducibility of our normative interests. It may indeed be no coincidence that various normative interests cluster around the body, i.e. around the very thing which is also the object of numerous non-normative concerns, without it being the case that these normative interests are grounded in these non-normative concerns. Rather each may be embedded in the other. The whole set of bodily interests – normative and non-normative – may come in a package whose elements can't either be pulled apart or arranged in order of explanatory priority.[20]

[20] I'm grateful to audiences at the Universities of Manchester, Birmingham, Sheffield, Oxford, London, Cambridge and Reading for comments on earlier versions of this paper and to the Leverhulme Foundation for the award of a Major Research Fellowship.

5

ENFORCEMENT RIGHTS AGAINST NON-CULPABLE NON-JUST INTRUSION

Peter Vallentyne

Abstract
I articulate and defend a principle governing enforcement rights in response to a non-culpable non-just rights-intrusion (e.g., wrongful bodily attack by someone who falsely, but with full epistemic justification, believes that he is acting permissibly). The account requires that the use of force reduce the harm from such intrusions and is sensitive to the extent to which the intruder is *agent-responsible* for imposing intrusion-harm

What enforcement rights does an agent have in response to a non-culpable non-just rights-intrusion (e.g., wrongful bodily attack by someone who falsely, but with full epistemic justification, believes that he is acting permissibly)? I shall defend a view according to which an agent has an enforcement right to intrude harmfully against another if the defensive intrusion (1) suitably *reduces non-just intrusion-harm* to the agent, (2) is no more harmful to the other than "reasonably" *necessary* to achieve the reduction, and (3) imposes intrusion-harm on the other that is *proportionate* in a specified manner to the reduction achieved. Moreover, although the proportionality restrictions decrease the more the other is *agent-responsible* for imposing intrusion-harm, they can be satisfied even if the other bears no such responsibility. Thus, there are enforcement rights against non-just intruders who are not responsible for the intrusion-harm they impose but not against innocent bystanders (who impose no intrusion-harm).

1. Background on the Problem: Intrusion, Unjust Infringement, and Enforcement Rights

I shall defend a principle governing the enforcement rights that individuals have in response to a non-just rights-intrusion, where this is understood as follows.

Developing Deontology, First Edition. Edited by Brad Hooker. Copyright © 2012 The Authors. Book compilation © 2012 Blackwell Publishing Ltd.

Individuals have, I shall assume, certain basic rights, such as certain rights of bodily integrity (e.g., the right not to be killed or assaulted). If, as I believe, individuals also have rights to compensation when their primary rights are wrongfully infringed, my discussion below also applies for the rights infringement of failing to provide owed compensation.[1]

A person's rights define certain conditions (e.g., that one not be hit), which, if not satisfied, raise the question of whether the right has been *intruded* upon. If rights are understood as protecting *choices*, then non-satisfaction of the conditions intrudes upon those rights if and only if it is done *without the valid permission of the right-holder*. Rights can, however, be understood as protecting *interests* – with non-satisfaction of the conditions being intrusions, for example, when they are against the interests of the right-holder.[2] I believe that a mixed view is plausible, but, for simplicity of presentation, I shall focus on the choice-protecting account.

The following terminology will be invoked below:

Intrusion: The conditions defined by rights are not satisfied by someone (the intruder) without permission of the right-holder.

Non-autonomous intrusion: The intrusion is not the result of a (sufficiently) autonomous choice of the intruder (e.g., behaviour of an infant) and thus is neither permissible nor impermissible (and neither just nor unjust).[3]

---

[1] I also believe that those who enforce rights against an unjust intruder – whether their own rights or those of others – are owed a financial debt by the intruder equal to the reasonable cost of providing enforcement services in question. Enforcement rights thus also apply to rights-intrusions that are failures to pay the enforcement costs of prior rights-intrusion.

[2] For superb discussion of the debate between choice-protecting and interest-protecting conceptions of rights, see Matthew H. Kramer, N. E. Simmonds, and Hillel Steiner, *A Debate over Rights* (Oxford: Oxford University Press, 1998).

[3] This terminology departs from that used by Judith Jarvis Thomson in *The Realm of Rights* (Cambridge, MA: Harvard University Press, 1990), pp. 366–69 and in 'Self-Defense', *Philosophy and Public Affairs* 20 (1991), pp. 300–302). She lumps non-autonomous intrusions along with infringements and allows that they can be violations. However, Michael Otsuka, in his 'Killing the Innocent in Self-Defense', *Philosophy and Public Affairs* 23 (1994), pp. 74–94, successfully argues that such non-autonomous intrusions cannot be violations (e.g., because rocks and bears can intrude upon rights but cannot act wrongly). It follows, I believe, that they cannot even be infringements, since such intrusions are not wrong even in the absence of special justificatory conditions. Hence, we need the more general notion of intrusion to cover non-autonomous intrusions.

Autonomous Intrusion: The intrusion is the result of an autonomous choice of the intruder (e.g., a normal adult strikes you) and is thus either permissible or impermissible (and either just or unjust).[4]

We can further distinguish between two kinds of autonomous intrusion: infringements and non-infringements. An *infringement* (or unjust intrusion) is an autonomous intrusion for which there is no *strong justification*, where the latter is a justification that is sufficient to ensure that the intrusion *does not wrong* the right-holder. For example, if I shoot an innocent bystander in the leg in order to save a million lives, I infringe her right not to be shot in the leg. By contrast, I do *not* infringe your right not to be shot, if I shoot you in the leg when this is the only way to stop you from wrongly killing me. In this case, there is a strong justification that establishes that you are not wronged.[5]

Among infringements (unjust intrusions), we can further distinguish between those that are *permissible (mere infringements)* and those that are *impermissible (violations)*. The difference is whether there is a *weak justification*, where this is a justification that is sufficient to ensure that the action *is not wrong* in virtue of the intrusion, but which is *not* strong enough to ensure that the intrusion does not wrong the right-holder. For example, if I kill an innocent bystander to save a million lives, I infringe her right not to be killed, but, if saving a million is enough to make the infringement permissible, then I merely infringe her right. By contrast, when I kill an innocent bystander just for fun, there is no weak justification for the infringement, and it is a violation (impermissible).

I shall address defence against non-just intrusions, which include both non-autonomous intrusions and unjust ones (i.e., infringements). This is part of a larger project in which I extend this to cover enforcement rights against those who *facilitate* (e.g.,

---

[4]   I use 'infringe' in the sense given by Thomson (e.g., *Realm of Rights*, p. 122) that leaves open whether the intrusion is permissible. Others reserve 'infringe' for cases of permissible intrusion. See, for example, Jeff McMahan, *Killing in War* (Oxford: Oxford University Press, 2009), p. 10 and Jules Coleman, 'Corrective Justice and Property Rights,' in *Property Rights* edited by Ellen Frankel Paul, Fred D. Miller, Jr., and Jeffrey Paul (Cambridge: Cambridge University Press, 1994), p. 29.

[5]   I am intruding upon your right because (I here assume for illustration) you have not completely forfeited your right not to be shot. For example, if I could avoid all harm simply by shooting in the air, then my shooting your body would wrong you (and this would not be so, if your right not to be shot had been completely forfeited).

aid and abet) non-just intrusions by others, and rights of third parties to defend the rights *of others*. In this paper, however, I shall consider only enforcement rights against an individual who is intruding upon the enforcer.

Enforcement rights are a bundle of rights possessed in virtue of some past, present, or future non-just rights-intrusion. They consist roughly of: (1) moral liberty-rights – perhaps protected by claim-rights against interference – to intrude against a person (e.g., injure or restrain), (2) moral powers to give others such liberty-rights (e.g., to help one exercise one's enforcement liberty-rights), (3) moral powers to acquire additional rights over that person or his property (e.g., to confiscate some of his property or rights over his labour in order to obtain compensation), and (4) moral powers to relinquish such rights (e.g., by pardoning). For simplicity, I shall focus on the liberty-right in (1), since this is the core right.

Like most people, I assume that there are some enforcement rights (and thus that radical pacifism is mistaken) but these rights are limited in some way (and thus that those who infringe rights do not typically forfeit all their rights).

I shall focus on the enforcement rights individuals have in the absence of a state. Although I believe that individuals initially (prior to any transfer, etc.) have the same enforcement rights in the presence of a state, I shall not attempt to defend that view here.[6]

2. Intrusion-Harm Reduction

Enforcement rights against another are determined, I shall argue, by the extent to which defensive intrusion would reduce, in certain ways, the intrusion-harms that the other would impose. Moreover, they depend on the extent to which the other is agent-responsible for such harm. In this section, I explain the notion of intrusion-harm to which I appeal.

Intrusion-harms are harms (i.e., loss of well-being) that are the result of a rights-intrusion (whether or not the intrusion is just). The harm you suffer when I take the last seat on the public bus is not an intrusion-harm, if you have no right against me that I not

---

[6]   For discussion, see, for example, Peter Vallentyne, 'Libertarianism and the State', *Social Philosophy and Policy*, 24 (2007): 187–205, and A. John Simmons, 'Philosophical Anarchism', in A. John Simmons, *Justification and Legitimacy* (Cambridge: Cambridge University Press, 2001), pp. 102–21.

take that seat. *Direct intrusion-harm* is the harm to the intruded-upon right-holder. *Indirect intrusion-harm* from a given intrusion is the harm to others (third parties; e.g., my wife's suffering when I am beaten up). Although I believe that the reduction of indirect intrusion-harm is relevant to the determination of enforcement rights against culpable intruders, it is not relevant to the condition that I defend for non-culpable intruders. Thus, all references to intrusion-harm should be interpreted as references to direct intrusion-harm.

The reduction of intrusion-harm is the central consideration in the approach that I develop below. Throughout, this harm is to be understood as long-term, and not just short-term, intrusion-harm. On the view that I propose, not all intrusion-harm, however, is relevant to the determination of enforcement rights. First, only *non-just* intrusion-harm is relevant. This is intrusion-harm from unjust intrusions (infringements) or from non-autonomous intrusions. It excludes intrusion-harms from just intrusions (e.g., the harm imposed on a criminal to stop her from killing others). Second, for defensive action against another, only *uncompensated* non-just intrusion-harm is relevant, where this is intrusion-harm for which compensation is owed but not provided. Intrusion-harm for which compensation is owed and provided is not relevant to the condition I defend. Finally, only *net* uncompensated non-just intrusion-harm is relevant, where this is net of any compensation that the agent owes the other. Thus, if the other imposes uncompensated intrusion-harm on the agent, but the agent owed the other some compensation, then the other's *net* uncompensated intrusion-harm to the agent is suitably reduced. For brevity, all references to intrusion-harm should be understood as references to *net uncompensated long-term* intrusion-harm. Enforcement rights, I shall argue, are determined by how well they reduce such intrusion-harm.

I assume throughout that the permissibility of actions depends on the objective facts at the time of action, and not merely on what the agent believes or should reasonably believe, nor on how things happen to turn out. I shall therefore appeal to *objective probabilities*, understood as propensities, of events happening. If determinism is true, these probabilities will all be zero or one, but, if indeterminism is true, then some of the probabilities will be intermediate values. Of course, the assumption of the existence of such objective probabilities is controversial, but I shall not defend it here. We shall therefore appeal to the *expected value*, based on *objective probabilities*, of the intrusion-harms imposed on someone by a given action. For example, if, relative to a given action that I might perform, there is a 30% chance of ten units of intrusion-harm to you and a 70% chance of only five units of intrusion-harm, then the expected value of the intrusion-harm to you that my action imposes is 6.5 (= .3 × 10 + .7 × 5). In what follows, then, the intrusion-harm imposed by a given action should be understood as the *objective expected value* of intrusion harm imposed by that action.

Before formulating and defending principles of enforcement rights against non-just intrusion, let me make two methodological comments. First, my goal is to *specify* reasonably fully a set of morally valid enforcement rights. Giving a reasonably full specification will involve a fair amount of complexity, and this will, no doubt, put off some readers. The main alternative approach is to specify simpler pro tanto principles and to leave open the messy business of how they interact. I believe that both kinds of approach are important and useful, but I prefer to attempt a reasonably full specification. Doing so has the disadvantage of complexity and of effectively ensuring that the principles are false in some respects. The advantage is that the very real complexity is grappled with and claims are specified carefully enough to be refutable. If all investigation were to end next week, then we should surely focus on the pro tanto approach. If, however, investigation is to continue for a much longer period, then the specificationist approach will be one useful way of making progress over time by uncovering specific errors. In any case, it is in this spirit that I advocate the principle that follows.

Second, I defend these principles as fundamental moral principles to be tested by whether they would be endorsed in reflective equilibrium. This is a matter both of their abstract plausibility and of the plausibility of their concrete implications. Readers should be forewarned, however, that, because I take abstract plausibility very seriously, some of the implications disagree significantly with common sense. I take this as a mark against the theory but not a conclusive one. The most plausible theory overall may indeed be rather revisionary.

3. Sufficient Conditions for Enforcement Rights against Non-Culpable Non-Just Intrusions

Throughout, let Agent be an agent who is intruding defensively and let Target be a person against whom she intrudes. Typically,

Target will be a possible intruder against Agent, but this need not be so. I shall defend the following principle:

Enforcement: In a given choice situation, Agent has a moral liberty, against Target, to perform a specific act of intrusion upon Target if each of the following conditions holds:

(1) **Harm Reduction**: Agent's intrusion against Target lowers the (expected value of net uncompensated direct) non-just intrusion-harm to Agent *by all others* compared with that value if Agent does not intrude upon Target in that choice situation;

(2) **Necessity**: Agent has no alternative action that (a) achieves or exceeds the above reduction in intrusion-harm to Agent, (b) involves no infringements of rights of individuals other than Target, (c) is no worse for Agent, and (d) is better for Target (i.e., leaves him better off);[7] and

(3) **Proportionality:** The intrusion-harm imposed is proportionate, as specified below, to the reductions achieved in intrusion-harm to Agent.

In this section, I explain, with some motivation, these three conditions and the resulting principle. In the next section, I defend the principle against objections that it is too strong. The principle supplies only sufficient conditions for enforcement rights and clearly needs to be strengthened in several ways, but I shall not undertake that project here.

The harm-reduction condition requires that Agent's intrusion against Target reduce non-just intrusion-harm to Agent. This includes unjust intrusion and as well as non-autonomous intrusion-harm, from Target and others. These aspects will be defended below. A more general, but still plausible, version of this condition would allow the relevant harm reduction also to include reductions in the intrusion-harm *to others* (and not merely to the Agent), but here I restrict my attention to the weaker condition.

The necessity condition is satisfied when no more harm is imposed on Target than is necessary to achieve or exceed the reduction in the expected value of the non-just intrusion-harms to Agent, without infringing the rights of others and without imposing further costs on Agent. It does not require that intrusion be a

---

[7]   I thank David Sobel for flagging an error in a previous formulation.

last resort in the sense of requiring that all other alternatives have been tried already. If the intrusion suitably reduces the expected unjust intrusions-harms to Agent, then Agent is at liberty to intrude as a first resort, as long as it involves no excessive or needless harm to Target. Although limiting significant intrusion to the last resort may be useful guide in practice, there is little reason to think that this is required in principle in the literal sense. It would limit defensive action far too much. I shall have little to say about the necessity clause in what follows.

The proportionality condition was referenced above, but it was not specified. The rough idea is that there are limits on the intrusion-harm that may be imposed in order to defend against a given intrusion-harm. For example, a common view is that it is normally excessive to kill someone to prevent him from stealing your chocolate bar. Specifying the exact limits, however, is quite difficult and requires considerable complexity. I do this below.

I shall not appeal to any *theoretical* notion of proportionality (about which there would be competing theories). Instead, I shall simply state some specific conditions that limit the harm that may be imposed on Target. I avoid the appeal to theoretical proportionality because I am sceptical that there is any interesting general theory of proportionality.[8] Because Enforcement invokes very specific proportionality conditions (to be specified below), it is, of course, much easier to refute than if it merely invoked a vague reference to proportionality (leaving open what that requires). I believe, however, that specificity (even if I get it wrong) will help us understand exactly what kind of 'proportionality' condition is required for enforcement rights.

In agreement with McMahan[9], I claim that the relevant proportionality condition is sensitive to Target's *responsibility* for intrusion-harm and for acting impermissibly. Throughout, responsibility is understood as agent-responsibility (also called attributive, outcome, or moral responsibility), as opposed to both causal responsibility and substantive moral responsibility (e.g., being morally liable to punishment, having duty to compensate). To be responsible for an outcome in this sense, the agent must be causally responsible for the outcome and the outcome must be

---

[8]   It's often not clear whether appeals to proportionality are meant to be appeals to a theoretical notion of proportionality or simply hand-waving that recognizes the need for greater specificity.

[9]   For example, McMahan, *Killing in War.*

'suitably reflective' of the agent's autonomous agency. There is much debate about what exactly determines when an individual is responsible for something, but it is clear that one can be causally responsible for harm without being responsible for it.[10] This is arguably so when: (1) one's *agency* was not involved at all (e.g., because an unforeseeable gust of wind blew one against the right-holder), (2) one's agency was involved but one's *autonomy* was radically impaired (e.g., the actions of psychotics or of someone in an extreme panic), (3) one was subject to irresistible duress (e.g., a highly credible threat that one's family will be tortured and killed if one does not perform the action), or (4) one's autonomous agency was involved but one *could not have known* that one's choice would have the specified result (e.g., one could not have known that the terrorist had rigged the light switch to set off the bomb). Although a fully adequate theory of responsibility would recognize that it comes in degrees (e.g., based on the above factors), for simplicity I shall generally treat responsibility as a binary concept.

Responsibility, it should be stressed, is relative to a specified outcome. One can be responsible for some outcomes (e.g., the foreseeable results within one's control) but not for others (e.g., those results that could not have been foreseen). In particular, one can be responsible for intrusion-harm (responsible for both intruding and for the resulting harm) without being responsible for acting impermissibly and vice-versa – even when one performs impermissible acts that impose intrusion-harm. An agent who deliberately shoots an innocent person in the arm can be responsible for the intrusion-harm, but she is not responsible for acting impermissibly if she could not have known that the person was innocent (e.g., if all available evidence strongly supported the view that the 'victim' was a criminal about to perform mass murder). Moreover, an agent who knowingly trespasses on a person's property can be responsible for acting impermissibly, but

---

[10] See, for example, John Martin Fischer and Mark Ravizza, *Responsibility and Control: A Theory of Moral Responsibility*, (Cambridge: Cambridge University Press, 1999), Peter Vallentyne, 'Brute Luck and Responsibility' *Politics, Philosophy & Economics* 7 (2008), pp. 57–80, and the many references in each. For simplicity in the present paper, I often assume that agents are fully responsible for the foreseen or reasonably foreseeable results of their autonomous choices. In 'Brute Luck and Responsibility', however, I defend the view that agents are responsible only for the (foreseeable) *probability shift* that their autonomous choices induce. This is a much more limited conception of responsibility.

she may not be responsible for the intrusion-harm (e.g., damage to very valuable flowers) if she could not have known about that impact.

I believe that the correct proportionality requirement is sensitive to both responsibility for intrusion-harm and to responsibility for acting impermissibly. In this paper, however, I only address defence against *non-culpable* intrusion-harm. This is intrusion-harm that results from an action for which the agent is *not* responsible for acting wrongly (e.g., because he could not have known that the action was impermissible). I thus address innocent (non-autonomous) threats and innocent aggressors but not culpable aggressors. I would argue that the proportionality requirements are radically weaker in the case where the intruder is culpable. That, however, is a topic for another paper.

The proportionality requirement that I shall defend is intermediate to two common extremal positions. A *strict liability* approach holds that there are no proportionality limits on the harm that one may impose on an unjust intruder, as long as the harms is necessary to avoid non-just intrusion-harm. Responsibility is deemed irrelevant. A *strict responsibility* approach holds that all harm is excessive (disproportionate) against non-just (and even unjust) intruders who are responsible neither for imposing any intrusion-harm nor for acting wrongly. The condition that I will defend agrees with the strict liability approach that proportionality often allows the imposition of intrusion-harm against a non-just intruder who is not responsible for any intrusion-harm. It also agrees, however, with the strict responsibility approach that the greater the responsibility for intrusion-harm the weaker the proportionality restrictions.

I shall defend the following schema, in conjunction with a specification of when a choice by Agent is Target-admissible:

> **Proportionality**: The (expected value of the net uncompensated direct) intrusion-harm to Target by Agent's intrusion is no greater than the largest intrusion-harm to Target imposed by one of Agent's Target-admissible choices.

The notion of a choice by Agent being Target-admissible is just a placeholder for a specification of the relevant conditions (to be given below). The key point to note here is that (1) any Target-admissible choice will satisfy Proportionality, and (2) choices that are not Target-admissible will also satisfy Proportionality as long as the intrusion-harm to Target is no greater than some Target-admissible choice.

What, then, are the requirements for Target-admissibility? Let us start with the case where Target is *not* responsible for any intrusion-harm, even though he is non-justly imposing intrusion-harm. Suppose that Target is about to turn on a light switch, and that, although he could not have known this, it will set off a bomb that will cause Agent a loss of ten units of well-being. Here, I stipulate that the Target-admissible choices include any choice by Agent that, relative her choices infringing no one else's rights, *minimizes the total* of Target's non-just intrusion-harm to Agent and Agent's intrusion-harm to Target. The idea is that the intrusion-harm to each matters equally, and any choice that suitably minimizes the total is Target-admissible. When combined with Proportionality, this entails that a choice by Agent is proportionate with respect to Target just in case it imposes no more intrusion-harm on Target than some choice by Agent that suitably minimizes the relevant combined intrusion-harm to the two of them.

To illustrate this, suppose that Agent's options are: (1) doing nothing and suffering a ten-unit non-just harm from Target (10-0 distribution of harms), (2) imposing a ten-unit intrusion-harm on Target and suffering no intrusion-harm from him (0-10), and (3) reducing the harm to herself to one unit by imposing a two-unit harm on Target (1-2). If these are the only feasible actions available to Agent, and none infringes the rights of others, then only the third option minimizes the total relevant intrusion-harm to the two of them (total of three units vs. total of ten for the other two options). Thus, only the third option is Target-admissible, and only the first and the third option are proportionate (since only they impose no more than two-units of intrusion-harm on Target). This treats the intrusion-harm to Target (who is not responsible for any intrusion-harm) on a par with the intrusion-harm to Agent.

Suppose now that Agent has a fourth option that infringes no one else's rights: to impose a one-unit intrusion-harm on Target and to reduce Target's intrusion-harm to Agent to five units (5-1). This does not minimize the total 'relevant' intrusion-harm to the two: its total is six and the second option has a total of three (one unit to Agent and two units to Target). Nonetheless, Proportionality against Target allows Agent to perform this fourth action, since the one-unit intrusion-harm to Target is less than the two-unit intrusion harm to him from the admissible total-minimizing second option.

Consider then the following full statement of Target-admissibility (where the second clause will be explained below):

> **Target-Admissible Choice (definition):** A choice by Agent is target-admissible just in case, for that choice, the sum of Agent's intrusion-harm to Target and Target's non-just intrusion-harm to Agent is no greater than: (1) the smallest feasible total, relative to Agent's choices that infringe no one else's rights, plus (2) the (expected value of) the unjust intrusion-harm to Agent by Target *for which Target is responsible for the harm*, if Agent does not intrude against Target.[11]

Above, we supposed that Target was not responsible for any of his non-just intrusion-harm. In that case, the second clause above is empty and the specification given corresponds to that introduced above. By contrast, where, in the absence of intrusion-against Target, Target would be responsible for imposing *n-units* of (unjust) intrusion-harm on Agent, clause (2) increases the limit, for Target-Admissibility, on the total relevant intrusion-harm for Target and Agent, from the minimum feasible total to that total *plus n-units*. More actions by Agent are deemed target-admissible, and typically the maximum intrusion-harm to Target allowed by proportionality is thereby increased. Consider, for example, the above three-option example, except that Target is fully responsible for the intrusion-harm of *ten units* that he would impose on Agent in the absence of defensive action. Here, the minimum total relevant intrusion-harm is (again) three, and so any action with a total relevant intrusion-harm of no more than *thirteen* (3 + 10) is admissible. Thus, unlike the original case, Proportionality judges it non-excessive for Agent to impose the ten-unit harm on Target to eliminate all harm to herself.

I shall now defend Enforcement based on these conditions.

---

[11] I intend this to be understood as holding when Target's actions will impose an unjust intrusion-harm on Agent and Target is responsible for this action imposing intrusion-harm *on someone*. Thus, it does not require that Target be aware that the intrusion-harm will be imposed on Agent. This issue, however, requires further attention.

4. A Defence

Enforcement is a relatively weak principle. It only provides sufficient (but not necessary) conditions for enforcement rights against
those non-justly intruding against the agent. I believe that it can be
strengthened to provide plausible necessary and sufficient conditions by (1) weakening the harm reduction requirement to take
into account reductions in non-just intrusion-harms *to others* (and
not merely the agent), and (2) extending the proportionality
requirements to cover *culpable* non-just intrusion harm (which I
believe would be radically weaker than those provided here for the
non-culpable case) and *facilitation* of intrusion-harm (aiding and
abetting). Here, however, I shall limit myself to defending Enforcement against objections that it is already too strong.[12]

A first objection to Enforcement is that it can judge Agent to be
at liberty to intrude defensively against Target even when Target
is responsible neither for any risk of impermissible intrusion nor
for any risk of intrusion-harm. Target may, for example, have
been unable to know that he was acting impermissibly and unable
to know that he was imposing any intrusion-harm. Indeed, the
intrusion may not even have been the result of an autonomous
choice (e.g., the wind may have unexpectedly blown Target's body
towards Agent). Enforcement can indeed judge that Agent has a
liberty of defensive intrusion in such cases. It is important to note,
however, that the proportionality clause in such cases is very strict.
It requires that the intrusion-harm imposed on Target be no
greater than that imposed by at least one of Agent's feasible
actions that, relative to her actions that infringe no one else's
rights, minimizes the sum of the Target's non-just intrusion-harm
to Agent and Agent's intrusion-harm to Target. Although it is not
judged excessive to impose a 10-unit intrusion-harm on Target
when this is the only way of eliminating his 10-unit intrusion-harm
to Agent, it is judged excessive when Agent has the option of
imposing a one-unit intrusion-harm and bearing eight units of
intrusion-harm from Target.[13]

---

[12] Due to space limitations, I do not address the concerns that the approach is
informationally demanding and that it presupposes the well-being is interpersonally
comparable.

[13] Enforcement thus agrees with Yitzhak Benbaji, 'Culpable Bystanders, Innocent
Threats, and the Ethics of Self-Defense', *Canadian Journal of Philosophy* 35 (2005): 585–622
that the relative sizes of the harm imposed and the harm prevented matter.

Of course, Enforcement's proportionality restriction will seem too weak to those who insist that all intrusion-harm is excessive against those who are not responsible for imposing unjust intrusion-harm (especially where the intrusion is not the result of an autonomous choice). Such individuals, it may be argued, are just as innocent as innocent bystanders who pose no threat of unjust intrusion-harm and they should be treated no differently. I agree that they are just as innocent. I deny that they may be treated only as an innocent bystander may be treated. Unlike innocent bystanders, innocent intruders are intruders. I am not here denying that responsibility is relevant for the liberty to intrude defensively. I fully agree that it is highly relevant. My claim is that, although responsibility for intrusion-harm can increase the maximum proportionate intrusion-harm, absence of such responsibility does not reduce it to zero.

Enforcement occupies a position between two more common positions with respect to responsibility for intrusion-harm. On the one hand, some argue that what matters is unjust (or perhaps non-just) intrusion-harm and not responsibility for unjust intrusion-harm. They claim that those who impose unjust intrusion-harm without being responsible for such may be treated the same as those who deliberately impose unjust intrusion-harm.[14] On the other hand, some argue that what matters is *responsibility* for unjust intrusion-harm. They claim that those who impose unjust intrusion-harm without being responsible for such should be treated the same as those who pose no threat of unjust intrusion-harm (e.g., innocent bystanders).[15] Enforcement holds that *both* non-just intrusion-harm and responsibility for intrusion-harm are relevant. Non-responsible intruders are *not* the same as innocent bystanders because they pose a risk of intrusion-harm. Non-responsible intruders are not, however, the same as those who deliberately impose the risk of intrusion-harm; they are not responsible for the risk that they impose. The proportionality clause reflects this dual sensitivity.

---

[14] See, for example, Thomson, 'Self-Defense'.

[15] See for example, Otsuka, 'Killing the Innocent in Self-Defense' and McMahan, *Killing in War* (e.g., pp. 170–181). It should be noted, however, that Otsuka, and to a lesser extent McMahan, focus on non-autonomous intrusions as opposed to autonomous intrusions for which the intruder is not responsible for acting unjustly or for imposing risk of intrusion-harm. For criticism, see Jonathan Quong, 'Killing in Self-Defense', *Ethics* 119 (2009): 507–537.

A second objection concerns that manner in which Enforcement makes proportionality depend on responsibility for (non-just) intrusion-harm. Relatively uncontroversially, it holds that the proportionality restrictions are generally weaker the greater the intrusion-harm for which Target is responsible. More controversially, it holds that the maximum admissible total relevant intrusion-harm is increased by the amount of the (non-just) intrusion-harm for Target will be responsible if Agent does not intrude against Target. This may seem arbitrary. There are an infinite number of ways in which responsibility for intrusion-harm might increase maximum proportionate intrusion-harm. Why is the above manner the correct one?

This is an excellent question and I have no compelling answer. Of course, if one simply appeals to the theoretical notion of proportionality, with no specification of what it requires, one does not confront the problem of apparent arbitrariness. My goal, however, is to be more specific so that such questions can be addressed directly. That, of course, does not guarantee that I have good answers! Still, two considerations provide some support for Enforcement's proportionality requirement. One is the abstract plausibility of increasing the maximum admissible relevant total intrusion-harm by the amount for intrusion-harm for which Target is responsible. This has greater abstract plausibility than appealing to 50%, 300%, or any other percentage. The other consideration in support of this view is that it gives relatively plausible concrete implications. Certainly, 100% is more plausible than .00001% or 10,000%. This leaves open a wide range of possibilities, but the abstract plausibility of 100% then provides special support for 100%. Of course, there may be a more plausible way of making proportionality depend on responsibility, but until one is specified, the proposed view has, I think, enough plausibility to be taken seriously. At a minimum, it should help promote the discovery of more plausible specifications.

A third objection to Enforcement is that it is too strong in that it can permit intrusion against an individual who has never intruded against another and for whom there is no danger of *imminent* intrusion. Indeed, it can permit defensive intrusion against those who *probably will never* intrude against anyone. This is because Enforcement appeals to a reduction in the *expected value* of Target's non-just intrusion-harms. This includes all such possible harms, weighted by their probabilities, that Target may produce now *and in the future.* Thus, Enforcement can recognize enforcement rights against Target when there is only a 1% chance of non-just intrusion-harm 10 years hence, with no chance of any intrusions before then. The principle, that is, can justify preventive attack, and not merely defensive action to intrusions already in progress and pre-emptive attack (in response to imminent intrusions). Many find this implausible.

To start, let us note that, although the harm-reduction condition holds that all future possible non-just intrusion-harm can ground enforcement rights, the proportionality condition limits the relevant impact. If Target has not yet made any autonomous choices that increase the chance of the future non-just intrusion-harm, he is not yet responsible for that harm (even if it is highly likely that he will impose it). Moreover, if Target has made some such choices, but they only slightly increase the chance of intrusion-harm, and he is suitably aware, then he is only slightly responsible for the intrusion-harm. Hence, the proportionality requirements will be fairly strict relative to the harm to Agent. Nonetheless, Enforcement will often allow some enforcement rights in such cases, given that the proportionality requirements allow some intrusion-harm against Target even when he is not responsible for the intrusion-harm that he non-justly imposes. Therefore, a weakened form of the objection remains.

Common sense is indeed sceptical of the permissibility of preventive attack, but I claim that common sense is mistaken in this regard. I see no difference in principle between an individual who is 90% likely to intrude in two years and one who is 90% likely to intrude in two minutes (with no other relevant differences). Of course, typically, one has more options available to stop intrusions two years hence than to stop intrusions two minutes hence. Thus, some just ways of stopping the latter will not be just ways of stopping the former (because of the necessity requirement). This, however, is merely a contingent difference. Temporal distance in the future as such seems irrelevant. It is the probabilities that matter.

One might agree that there is no principled difference between imminent intrusions and distant intrusions and simply insist that defensive intrusion is justified in neither case. Only intrusions that have *already* taken place, or, less restrictively, are *100% certain* (which could include some future ones), one might argue, justify a defensive response. This view, however, takes an excessively limited view of enforcement rights. We do not have to wait for an intrusion to take place or be 100% certain in order to take just defensive action. Surely, we are sometimes permitted to intrude defensively against 99% or even 90% chance of intrusion. Moreover, there is no reason in principle to limit defensive action to cases where the intrusions are highly likely. It also depends on how large the intrusion-harm will be.[16] Of course, in practice, our knowledge is highly limited, and it may well be advisable in general to limit defensive intrusion to cases that are imminent, highly likely, and/or in process.

A fourth objection to Enforcement is that it holds that intrusion-harm may be imposed on Target in order to reduce the non-just intrusion-harm *from others*. This is because the harm reduction condition only requires a reduction in the total non-just intrusion-harm to Agent *by anyone*. This need not involve any reduction in non-just intrusion-harm from Target. It may simply deter others from non-justly intruding against Agent, or even just reduce the intrusion-harm to her when they do. It is important to keep in mind, however, that the proportionality requirement rules out imposing any intrusion-harm on someone who does not impose any non-just intrusion-harm (innocent bystanders). Thus, only those who are imposing non-just intrusion-harm are liable to being used as means to deter others. Moreover, if they bear little or no responsibility for such intrusion-harm, the proportionality requirements will very radically limit the harm that may be imposed on them for that purpose. For those that bear significant responsibility for non-just intrusion-harm, Enforcement does indeed justify using them as means for reducing non-just intrusion-harm to Agent from others, but they are not being used merely as a means, since even here the proportionality and necessity requirements hold. Moreover, given that in this case Target is (autonomously) unjustly intruding and responsible for significant intrusion-harm, it seems reasonable that he becomes liable to being used to reduce intrusion-harm to Agent.

A fifth objection to Enforcement is that it can judge that one is at liberty to intrude against Target even though this *increases* non-just intrusion-harms *to others*. This is so because Enforcement

---

[16] For further defenses of preventive attack, see Thomson, *Realm of Rights* (p. 364); Thomas Hurka, 'Proportionality in the Morality of War', *Philosophy and Public Affairs* 33 (2005): 34–66; David Rodin, *War and Self-Defense* (Oxford: Oxford University Press, 2002), p. 41; Gerhard Øverland, 'Killing Soldiers', *Ethics and International Affairs* 20 (2006): 455–75; and Michael Doyle, *Striking First: Preemption and Prevention in International Conflict* (Princeton: Princeton University Press, 2008), p. 474.

has no conditions concerning the impact on others. Here, we need to consider two cases: where Target is not acting permissibly and where he is. An example of the former case is where Agent can obtain a small reduction in unjust relevant intrusion-harm to herself, but enraged Target will then go off and impose enormous impermissible intrusion-harms on each of many other people. It may seem implausible that Agent is permitted to defend herself in such a case. The reply, however, is simple. I am not claiming that Agent is so permitted. I am only claiming that she has a liberty-right *against Target* to defend herself. Such defence may be unjust or impermissible because it infringes rights that *others* hold against Agent. My only claim is that Target is not wronged (i.e., Agent has a liberty-right to so defend herself).

Consider, then, the second case, where Target is *acting permissibly* in unjustly intruding upon Agent. Target's action infringes, but does not violate, Agent's rights. For example, perhaps Agent is fully innocent but Target's attacking her is the only way of saving a billion lives. Here, Agent's liberty, against Target, to defend against Target's attack is more difficult to justify. Still, given that Agent is innocent and Target is infringing her rights, it is hard to see why Agent would not have some enforcement rights against Target. This is not, however, to say that it is permissible for Agent to exercise those rights. She may owe duties to others that she not do so. Indeed, this is the most plausible explanation. Given that a billion lives are at stake, those individuals may have a claim-right that she not defensively intrude against Target (similar to the situation in which she promised her mother not to do so). Such defensive intrusion may be impermissible, but that does not show that she does not have enforcement rights *against Target*. Obviously, the issue is complex, but I shall not undertake further defence here.

A sixth objection is that variations among individuals in the capacity for well-being will generate variations in the strength of enforcement rights. This arises both because the harm-reduction clause is sensitive to whether a given intrusion harms Agent at all and because the proportionality clause is sensitive to the magnitudes of the intrusion-harms to Agent and to Target. All else being equal, those with greater vulnerability to loss of well-being will have stronger enforcement rights and stronger protections against intrusion. Intuitively, this seems inappropriate.

In reply, let us start with the case where an individual is *not responsible* for his greater than average vulnerability to loss of well-being (i.e., it is a matter of brute luck and not cultivated). Here, it seems quite appropriate for enforcement rights to be sensitive to the actual intrusion-harm. Next, suppose, as is plausible, that individuals are at least partially responsible for their specific vulnerability to loss of well-being from intrusions. We shall consider the case where the individual is Agent and the case where the individual is Target. For the former, there again seems to be little reason not to take their actual harm to be the relevant harm. Suppose that Agent devotes her life to playing the piano well and, as a result, she would lose much more well-being from damage to her little finger than most. Still, if Target is non-justly intruding upon her little finger, surely the strength of Agent's enforcement rights depends on how much actual well-being she can protect. She may not be entitled to any help in promoting her cultivated interests, but surely she is entitled to protect them when non-justly intruded upon.

The more difficult case is the second one, where Target is responsible for having a greater vulnerability to loss of well-being. Here, it may seem implausible that he could make himself less liable to defensive attack against his non-just intrusion (especially if unjust) merely by cultivating greater vulnerability to intrusion-harm. I believe that this is indeed implausible in the case of *culpable* non-just intrusions (i.e., where the agent is responsible for acting wrongly), but I am not addressing such cases in this paper. Here, we are addressing only non-culpable non-just harmful intrusion, and there are three sub-cases: non-autonomous intrusion, autonomous intrusion with no responsibility for any intrusion-harm, and autonomous intrusion with responsibility for intrusion-harm. For the first two sub-cases, there is no reason to treat them differently from the case of Agent above. In all these cases, the individual is non-culpable and not responsible for any intrusion-harm. His actual well-being is what matters. (Keep in mind that I here appeal to the correct account of well-being. I do not assume welfarism.) The third case, where the intruder is responsible for intrusion-harm, is not as obviously the same, but, given that he is non-culpable, even here the focus on actual well-being seems appropriate. Although he is acting unjustly, and perhaps impermissibly, he is not responsible for so acting (e.g., due to unavoidable ignorance). Obviously, this is a complex issue that requires a more elaborate discussion, but I shall not pursue it further here.

A seventh objection is that Enforcement fails to distinguish between intrusions upon *rights to one's person* and intrusions upon *rights to external things.* Even if Enforcement is correct about the former, it might be argued that it is too strong for intrusions against the latter. Enforcement does indeed lump together intrusion-harms from all kinds of intrusions, but this, I claim, is correct. What matters is the harm *to persons* from intrusions. It does not matter what kind of intrusion produced a given intrusion-harm. The large intrusion-harm from the destruction of a cherished object is far more important to protect than the trivial intrusion-harm of a light punch. One might insist, however, that, because intrusion-harms from intrusions against rights to external property can typically be rectified whereas intrusions against rights in one's person often cannot, enforcement rights are weaker with respect to external things.[17] I fully agree that intrusions-harms that are not fully compensable should be treated differently from those that are. Enforcement is sensitive to this because it focuses on net *uncompensated* intrusion-harms. Intrusion-harms that will be voluntarily, or forcibly, fully compensated provide no justification for defensive intrusion. This provides, however, no reason to treat intrusions against property as fundamentally different from those against persons. Some intrusions against rights to personal external property may be not rectifiable (e.g., one's favourite drawing by one's dead child), and some intrusions against rights to one's person (e.g., a gentle push) are fully rectifiable. What matters is whether the harms will be fully compensated, not the nature of the intrusion.

Obviously, there are other aspects of Enforcement to which one might object, but enough has been said, I hope, to give at least the general shape of Enforcement some plausibility.

5. Conclusion

I have formulated and partially defended a sufficient condition for enforcement rights against non-culpable non-just intrusions. I believe the condition can be strengthened to a necessary and sufficient condition by (1) weakening the harm reduction requirement to include non-just intrusion-harm to others (and not just to

---

[17] See Rodin, *War and Self-Defense,* p. 44, for a defense of this view, although his claim is the weaker claim that the *lethal* use of force is limited to the defense of intrusion against persons.

Agent), and (2) weakening the proportionality requirement so that higher limits are set for those responsible facilitating non-just intrusion-harm by others and radically higher limits are set for those who culpably intrude. That, however, is a topic for another paper.

I have no doubt that Enforcement, given its specificity, is mistaken in many ways. My hope is that the mistakes are correctible within the general approach, but I will not be surprised if certain fundamental aspects of the approach turn out to be mistaken. I believe, however, that the approach is promising enough to be worthy of further consideration. At a minimum, exposing its errors should be instructive.[18]

[18] For comments on a significantly different precursor of this paper, I thank Justin McBrayer, Eric Roark, and Alan Tomhave. For comments on this paper, I thank the audiences at the University of Reading and Washington University, Dani Attas, Crystal Allen, Jeremy Davis, Joel Dittmer, Kim Ferzan, Seth Lazar, Xiaofei Liu, Jeff McMahan, Iddo Porat, Jonathan Quong, Brandon Schmidly, David Sobel, Hillel Steiner, Eric Roark, Jon Trerise, Bas van der Vossen, and Leo Yan.

6

DOES MORAL IGNORANCE EXCULPATE?

Elizabeth Harman

Abstract
Non-moral ignorance can exculpate: if Anne spoons cyanide into
Bill's coffee, but thinks she is spooning sugar, then Anne may be
blameless for poisoning Bill. Gideon Rosen argues that moral ignorance can also exculpate: if one does not believe that one's action
is wrong, and one has not mismanaged one's beliefs, then one is
blameless for acting wrongly. On his view, many apparently blameworthy actions are blameless. I discuss several objections to Rosen.
I then propose an alternative view on which many agents who act
wrongly are blameworthy despite believing they are acting morally
permissibly, and despite not having mismanaged their moral
beliefs.[1]

Gideon Rosen has argued for the following Broad Conclusion:

A person who acts wrongly is blameworthy for so acting only if
the action itself is a case of clear-eyed *akrasia* or the action
results from a case of clear-eyed *akrasia*.[2]

While the Broad Conclusion is stated in terms of *akrasia*, its main
upshot is regarding *moral knowledge* and *moral ignorance*. An akratic
action is one done in the belief that one should act differently.

---

[1] For helpful comments on drafts of this paper, I am grateful to Charles Beitz, Peter
Graham, Alexander Guerrero, Adam Hosein, and audiences at the CUNY Graduate Conference, the Inland Northwest Philosophy Conference, the New York Society for Women in
Philosophy, Princeton University's Program in Law and Public Affairs, Rutgers University,
the University of Texas at Austin, and Yale Law School. I also thank the participants in my
spring 2009 graduate seminar.
[2] Gideon Rosen, 'Skepticism about Moral Responsibility,' *Philosophical Perspectives* 18
(2004), 295–313; the paper uses what I am calling the Broad Conclusion to argue for a
further claim, that we never have *knowledge* that someone is blameworthy for an action.
(This follows from the further premise that we never have knowledge that clear-eyed
akrasia has occurred.)
   While Michael Zimmerman ('Moral Responsibility and Ignorance,' *Ethics* 107 (1997),
410–426) and Susan Wolf ('Moral Saints,' *Journal of Philosophy* 79 (1982), 419–439) make
arguments that are in some respects similar to Rosen's, I will focus on Rosen's argument.

Someone who acts wrongly while ignorant that he should act differently is not acting *akratically*. The Broad Conclusion implies that someone who acts wrongly without believing that he should act differently is blameworthy only if his action results from a case of clear-eyed *akrasia*: that is, only if it results from some earlier behavior performed in the full belief that it should not be performed. On Rosen's view, all blameworthiness has its root in wrong behavior that was performed while the agent knew she should act differently.

Others have shown that Rosen's argument does not succeed in establishing the Broad Conclusion. However, Rosen's argument may still seem to establish a narrower conclusion which would imply that many ordinary apparently blameworthy actions are in fact blameless. I will argue that Rosen's narrower conclusion is false, and I will develop a view of blameworthiness on which these ordinary apparently blameworthy actions are indeed blameworthy.

Section 1 sketches Rosen's argument for his Broad Conclusion. Section 2 explains some compelling points made by Alexander Guerrero, Michelle Moody-Adams, and William FitzPatrick, which undermine parts of Rosen's argument, and outlines the narrower conclusion that Rosen's argument may seem to establish after these points are taken into account. Along the way, section 2 also offers a new objection to Rosen's argument and raises an objection to a claim of FitzPatrick's. Section 3 argues that the narrower conclusion is nevertheless significantly revisionary about blameworthiness: it implies that many ordinary apparently blameworthy actions are in fact blameless. Section 4 proposes a view on which these actions are indeed blameworthy. Sections 5 clarifies the proposed view and defends it in the face of some objections. Section 6 offers a way of understanding the dispute between the view I propose and Rosen's view, and offers my most important objection to Rosen's paper.

1. Rosen's Argument

Let's begin with the natural thought that ignorance of non-moral matters can exculpate. Suppose Anne spoons some cyanide into Bill's coffee, but she does not know it is cyanide: she believes that she is spooning sugar. It seems that Anne is blameworthy for poisoning Bill only if she is blameworthy for her ignorance. If we stipulate that Anne is not blameworthy for her ignorance, then it seems Anne is not blameworthy for poisoning Bill.

Rosen draws a general lesson from this case:

Lesson:
A wrong action (or omission) done from ignorance is not a locus of *original responsibility*; rather, it is at most a locus of *derivative responsibility*: if the agent is blameworthy for the wrong action (or omission), he is so blameworthy only in virtue of being blameworthy for the ignorance.[3]

To understand the notions of *original responsibility* and *derivative responsibility*, Rosen offers the example of someone who goes berserk and destroys his hotel room while high on a drug: his actions are not loci of *original responsibility*, but they may be loci of *derivative responsibility*, in that he may be blameworthy for them by being blameworthy for having taken the drug.

Rosen furthermore claims:

An agent is blameworthy for some ignorance only if he has behaved in ways that constitute a violation of our *procedural epistemic obligations* and this behavior has resulted in his ignorance.

Rosen points out that we are obligated to take precautions against harming others (and against other wrongdoing) and that among the precautions we are obligated to take are epistemic precautions. He writes, 'these procedural obligations are always obligations to *do* (or to refrain from doing) certain things: to ask certain questions, to take careful notes, to stop and think, to focus one's attention in a certain direction, etc. The procedural obligation is not itself an obligation to know or believe this or that. It is an obligation to *take steps* to ensure that when the time comes to act, one will know what one ought to know' (301). Rosen stresses that we are not obligated to take all the precautions that we could take, and he suggests that we are obligated to act as a 'person of ordinary prudence' would act. I will use the expression 'mismanagement of one's opinion' to describe any violation of our procedural epistemic obligations.

---

[3] Note that 'from ignorance' here means from a position of ignorance; it does not require that the ignorance is a cause of the action.

Rosen claims blameworthiness for ignorance can only arise from blameworthiness for *behavior* to do with the management of one's beliefs because he claims a belief itself cannot be a locus of original blameworthiness; he claims beliefs are not voluntary in the way that any locus of original blameworthiness must be voluntary; he says that a belief is something that 'simply happens in me or to me' (302).

Rosen also claims:

> Every instance of morally wrong behavior (whether an action or an omission) is either a case of behavior from ignorance or a case of clear-eyed *akrasia*.

In a case of wrong action (or omission) due to clear-eyed *akrasia*, a person performs a wrong action (or an omission) while aware that she has most reason to act otherwise. In any other case, Rosen claims, the action in question is done from ignorance, because it is done at least from ignorance *that* one has most reason to act otherwise. (Thus, Rosen claims that even someone who knows she is acting wrongly but does not know that morality is overriding – and so, that she has most reason to act otherwise – is acting in ignorance. I will not address this implication of his views.)

What emerges from the three claims I have highlighted is the following. A wrong action (or omission) is either a case of clear-eyed *akrasia* or it is an action (or omission) from ignorance. A wrong action (or omission) from ignorance is not a locus of original responsibility; if it is blameworthy then it is blameworthy only in virtue of blameworthiness for an earlier behavior which constitutes violation of procedural norms in the management of one's beliefs. This earlier behavior is similarly either itself clear-eyed *akrasia* or done from ignorance, in which case it is blameworthy only if an earlier behavior is blameworthy, which is itself blameworthy only if it is clear-eyed akrasia or it results from blameworthy behavior.

Rosen illustrates the application of his principles with an example of a surgeon who has type A blood transfused into a patient who has type B blood. The surgeon forgets to double-check the chart, although double-checking at such a time is standard procedure. The surgeon's ignorance that the patient has type B blood means she is not originally responsible for her transfusion order. But she may be derivatively responsible, if she is responsible for her failure to double-check the chart. When she forgot to double-check the chart, she was not thinking about the chart, and she did not know she should check the chart. So her failure to check the chart was itself in ignorance of the fact that she should do so, and she is blameworthy for that only if she is blameworthy for some earlier behavior which resulted in her ignorance that she should check the chart. If she tends to be forgetful about checking such charts, then she should have asked someone to remind her. But if this is a case of forgetfulness that was not particularly foreseeable, then she is not blameworthy.

I will also mention how the argument applies to a case Rosen discusses in an earlier paper.[4] Consider an ancient slaveholder, who believes it is permissible to keep slaves. Ancient slavery was not race-based and was not based on the belief that some group of people was inferior to another group; rather, slaves had been captured in battle. Being a slave was seen as an unfortunate state that in principle anyone might have found himself in. So it is plausible that a person could know all the non-moral facts and yet believe that this slavery was permissible. At this time, while everyone thought it was awful to *be* a slave, no one suggested that it was wrong to keep slaves. Is the ancient slaveholder blameworthy for keeping slaves? He is not originally blameworthy, because of his moral ignorance. Is he blameworthy for his ignorance? It does not seem he has been negligent in the management of his opinion. He doesn't ignore arguments against slavery: none are offered to him. He thinks about morality as much as any ordinary person. On Rosen's view, the slaveholder is blameless because he is ignorant that his behavior is morally wrong and he has not violated any procedural norms in the management of his beliefs.

2. Objections to Rosen's Argument

I will discuss four objections to Rosen's argument. The first objection is due to Alexander Guerrero; he raised it as an objection to an earlier paper of Rosen's. The second objection is new; it emerges from consideration of the first objection. The third objection emerges from consideration of a paper by Michelle Moody-Adams; her paper was published before Rosen's papers on

---

[4]   Gideon Rosen, 'Culpability and Ignorance,' *Proceedings of the Aristotelian Society* CIII (2003), Part 1.

this topic but it addresses the same issues. The fourth objection is a generalization of points made both in Moody-Adams's paper and in a paper of William FitzPatrick's; FitzPatrick's paper is addressed to the argument of Rosen's that I have presented. In the course of discussing FitzPatrick's paper, I will object to a claim he makes about the nature of a certain class of cases of ordinary blameworthiness. At the end of this section, I will describe the narrower conclusion that Rosen's argument might seem to establish even in the face of these four objections.

The first objection is a generalization of an objection made by Guerrero.[5]

Let's consider again the case of Anne, who poisons Bill by spooning cyanide into his coffee. Anne believes she is spooning sugar, and is blameless for her false belief. Anne is blameless for poisoning Bill. Rosen takes the lesson of cases like this to be that an action done from *ignorance* is not a locus of original responsibility. However, that is the wrong lesson. Consider a variant of the case. Alice spoons cyanide into Bob's coffee. Alice is *ignorant* that she is spooning cyanide, in that she lacks a belief that it is cyanide; rather, she has .5 credence that it is sugar and .5 credence that it is cyanide. It is false that Alice is blameworthy for spooning the cyanide only if she is blameworthy for her ignorance. Rather, Alice's spooning of the cyanide is a locus of original responsibility: she is directly blameworthy for poisoning Bob. (In a later paper, Rosen grants that in cases like that of Alice and Bob, ignorance does not in any way exculpate.[6])

The following lesson might be drawn: it is not *ignorance* that can exculpate, but *false belief*. Only the following weaker lesson seems warranted by reflection on cases of action from non-moral ignorance:

Weaker Lesson:
If an agent acts wrongly while falsely believing that p, and if p were true then her action would be morally permissible, *then* the agent's action is not a locus of original responsibility: if she is blameworthy for acting, then she is so blameworthy only in virtue of being blameworthy for her false belief.

---

[5]   Alexander Guerrero, 'Don't Know, Don't Kill: Moral Ignorance, Culpability, and Caution,' *Philosophical Studies* 136 (2007), 59–97. I omit discussion of Guerrero's complex paper; the example I present makes the point his paper presses, but it is not his example.
[6]   Gideon Rosen, 'Kleinbart the Oblivious and Other Tales of Ignorance and Responsibility,' *Journal of Philosophy* 105 (2008), 591–610, footnote 14.

(Note that I do not endorse this principle; I simply claim that the Weaker Lesson is a better inference to draw from the cases than the Lesson Rosen does draw, which is not plausible in light of the cases.[7])

The upshot is that the generality of Rosen's conclusion is substantially limited. Note that Rosen claimed:

> Every instance of morally wrong behavior (whether an action or an omission) is either a case of behavior from ignorance or a case of clear-eyed *akrasia*.

But in conjunction with the Weaker Lesson, to establish the Broad Conclusion, Rosen would need this claim instead:

> Every instance of morally wrong behavior (whether an action or an omission) is either a case of behavior from false belief in p, such that if p is true then the behavior is permissible, or a case of clear-eyed *akrasia*.

This claim is false. Many instances of morally wrong behavior do not involve clear-eyed *akrasia* because the agent lacks a firm view about whether his behavior is wrong; such behavior involves lack of true moral belief – and hence, *moral ignorance* – without involving moral *false belief*. It now seems that, contra Rosen's original argument, such behavior may well be a locus of original responsibility. Just as Alice's uncertainty regarding whether she was spooning cyanide did not undermine her being originally responsible for so acting, similarly mere uncertainty regarding whether one is acting wrongly does not undermine original responsibility for one's action. If someone acts wrongly while genuinely unsure whether her action is wrong, we need not investigate whether she is blameworthy for being unsure to know whether she is blameworthy: she may well be blameworthy simply for doing what she did, which she believed might well be wrong. (Of course she may not be blameworthy if there are other exculpatory factors, for example if she is under the influence of a powerful drug. Or she may not be blameworthy if she has no option available to her that she is sure is morally permissible.)

---

[7] In footnote 21, I discuss another way Rosen might revise the lesson in response to the first objection.

The second objection emerges from what we have learned so far. Rosen takes his argument to apply to cases of wrongful omissions, including cases of *forgetting* to do something; he treats such forgettings as involving ignorance. Consider the following case. A doctor forgets to check a chart and fails to see that a patient is allergic to a common antibiotic; she prescribes the antibiotic, and the patient dies.[8] On Rosen's view, in this case, the failure to check is not a case of clear-eyed *akrasia*, because the doctor is not thinking about whether to check. Thus the failure to check is not a locus of original responsibility. Thus the doctor is blameworthy only if there is some earlier behavior which is an instance of clear-eyed *akrasia*. Let's stipulate there is not.

Let's apply the lessons of the prior discussion. What first emerged is that, if anything, it is *false beliefs* that exculpate. Does the doctor have a false belief that it is okay not to check the chart? No! Indeed, she believes that, in cases like this, she should check the chart. Applying the Weaker Lesson does not vindicate the claim that the doctor is blameless.

Once we see that it is only plausible that *false belief* exculpates, not that *ignorance* does, we will cease to see Rosen's arguments as applying to cases of omissions of actions due to failure to think about or attend to certain facts, including moral requirements. While such cases of forgetting to do things do involve a failure to attend to certain facts, they do not involve the formation of other beliefs that falsely imply one's actions are permissible.[9]

(Note that the second objection does not require that a doctor in such a case is blameworthy; I merely claim that Rosen's line of thought provides no argument that she is blameless.)

The second objection implies a specific conclusion about Rosen's discussion of blameworthiness for ignorance. Rosen says that one is blameworthy for one's ignorance only if one is blameworthy for violating certain procedural norms. He furthermore points out that often one will not have thought about these norms as one violated them. This, he claims, means that one is violating the norms in ignorance, and thus one is not originally responsible for the violation. But this is to treat the

---

[8] Note: this is a different case from the earlier case of the doctor who does not double-check a patient's blood type.

[9] It might be objected that the doctor who forgets to check the chart has a general implicit belief that she is not currently doing anything wrong, and that this is enough to render her action blameless. I respond to this objection in section 6.

violation of the norms in the same way that he treats the doctor who forgets to check the chart for allergies. It may be true that people who violate procedural epistemic norms are not attending to the norms as they violate them; but it is not true that people in such cases have false beliefs to the effect that failure to perform the behavior the norms require is permissible. Rosen's argument does not support his claim that many cases of failure to observe procedural epistemic norms are not loci of original blameworthiness.

I will now turn to the third and fourth objections to Rosen's argument. Both objections arise out of Michelle Moody-Adams's insights.[10] Moody-Adams is concerned to rebut the view that people are blameless for wrong actions which are seen, in their cultures, as morally permissible (or even required). She points out that many such mistaken moral views licensed practices which were of great benefit to those who committed the moral crimes in question. Just as in an individual case, a person may fail to realize something out of *motivated ignorance*, because she does not want to realize it, similarly each individual within a whole group of privileged people may fail to realize that their practices are wrong out of motivated ignorance. If a cultural practice continues and is accepted in a society not simply because people are *ignorant* of its moral wrongness, but because people *don't want to see* its moral wrongness, the ignorance looks less innocent and the practice is more plausibly blameworthy.

The third objection is this:

> An individual may be blameworthy for a false moral belief, although he has not violated any procedural norms to do with the management of his opinion, if his false moral belief is due to *motivated ignorance*.

I think this objection is persuasive, but I will note that it relies on the claim that motivated ignorance is blameworthy, which is no doubt a controversial claim. Rosen would respond to the third objection by saying that the third objection attributes blameworthiness for believing, which is something that happens to one, not something one does.

---

[10] Michelle Moody-Adams, 'Culture, Responsibility, and Affected Ignorance,' *Ethics* 104 (1994), 291–309.

The third objection is not explicitly made by Moody-Adams. Her discussion inspires the point, but she is not committed to it. What she commits herself to is a different claim, which is the fourth objection I will discuss:

A person may be blameworthy for ignorance which arises out of mismanagement of her opinion, although this mismanagement did not involve any clear-eyed *akrasia* (nor is there an earlier instance of *akrasia*).

Moody-Adams points out that if someone has false moral beliefs which benefit him, he may well avoid information and reflection which would lead his false beliefs to be revealed as false: he may be motivated to *protect* his false beliefs. He may not be aware that this is the correct account of his behavior, and so he may not be aware that he is violating any procedural norms to do with the management of his opinion, and so he may not be engaged in any clear-eyed *akrasia*.

William FitzPatrick[11] also presses the fourth objection, though he does not focus only on motivated ignorance.

FitzPatrick describes the following case, which is based on the movie 'It's a Wonderful Life'; it is an expansion of a case Rosen discusses. Mr. Potter is a businessman who decides to close down a business, which will result in many jobs being lost. Mr. Potter has thought about the morality of his action, and has concluded that his action is 'permissively aggressive' although the action is really 'reprehensibly ruthless.' Rosen's view implies that Mr. Potter is blameworthy for acting only if he is blameworthy for his ignorance. FitzPatrick argues that this must be a case in which the agent mismanaged his beliefs, because it is not a 'hard case' in which someone thinking carefully about how he should act might get it wrong. For Rosen, the question becomes: did Mr. Potter's mismanagement of his beliefs involve an instance of clear-eyed *akrasia*? If so, Mr. Potter may be blameworthy. If not, Mr. Potter's mismanagement was out of ignorance and then we must ask whether he is blameworthy for that ignorance. Fitz-Patrick disagrees with Rosen: he thinks that Mr. Potter can be blameworthy for the mismanagement of his beliefs even in the

---

[11]   William FitzPatrick, 'Moral Responsibility and Normative Ignorance: Answering a New Skeptical Challenge,' *Ethics* 118 (2008), 589–613.

absence of clear-eyed *akrasia*. FitzPatrick says the right question is whether Mr. Potter can have been *reasonably expected* not to mismanage his beliefs; furthermore, FitzPatrick concludes, there are versions of the case in which Mr. Potter *can* reasonably have been expected not to mismanage his beliefs. Mr. Potter's mismanagement of his beliefs may have been an instance of an exercise of a vice of Mr. Potter's. He may have been overconfident, arrogant, dismissive, lazy, dogmatic, incurious, self-indulgent, or contemptuous (these are FitzPatrick's adjectives) in not taking adequately seriously, and in not adequately exploring, alternative moral viewpoints regarding business ethics. If Mr. Potter's ignorance resulted from the exercise of any of these vices, then, FitzPatrick claims, Mr. Potter is blameworthy despite there being no instance of clear-eyed *akrasia*. Thus, FitzPatrick thinks this case establishes the claim made by the fourth objection:

> A person may be blameworthy for ignorance which arises out of mismanagement of her opinion, although this mismanagement did not involve any clear-eyed *akrasia* (nor is there an earlier instance of *akrasia*).

The idea is that Mr. Potter may have been, for example, *overconfident* in coming to his beliefs, though this expression of that vice did not result from some earlier behavior which was an instance of clear-eyed akrasia. Nevertheless, FitzPatrick contends, Mr. Potter is blameworthy.[12]

The fourth objection's claim is controversial. As pressed by both Moody-Adams and FitzPatrick, the fourth objection is supported by the description of a case and the claim that the agent is blameworthy for his mismanagement of his beliefs. Moody-Adams says that mismanagement of beliefs which is in fact due to a desire not to know the truth (though this may be ill understood by the agent himself) is blameworthy, and FitzPatrick says that mismanagement of beliefs which constitutes the exercise of a vice is blameworthy. The claims are compelling, I think. But

---

[12] FitzPatrick makes another objection to Rosen, which is an objection to Rosen's argument *from* what I call the Broad Conclusion to the further claim that we never have *knowledge* that someone is blameworthy for an action. FitzPatrick argues compellingly that we do often have knowledge that *akrasia* has occurred, and so that the Broad Conclusion does not imply the further claim.

Rosen would not be convinced. To FitzPatrick, Rosen would respond that most of the vices in question, properly understood, involve the *false belief* that S is not mismanaging his beliefs. One's time for moral consideration is not limitless, so it is not a good idea (nor morally required) to consider every idle moral worry. Consider the vices of overconfidence, arrogance, dismissiveness, dogmatism, incuriosity and contemptuousness. These vices seem to involve the *belief* that the other views in question aren't worth taking seriously. These are *false beliefs* in this case, but Rosen would say that, in virtue of Mr. Potter's having such beliefs, his mismanagement of his opinion is out of ignorance (indeed, is vindicated by these false beliefs). The disagreement between FitzPatrick and Rosen amounts to a standoff over the case FitzPatrick describes. Rosen will simply deny FitzPatrick's claims about the case. But others may be moved by the case and see it as showing that Rosen's argument fails.

In discussing Mr. Potter, FitzPatrick makes an argument to which I will now object. FitzPatrick argues that an immoral businessman such as Mr. Potter must have mismanaged his beliefs – that is, violated a procedural epistemic norm – because the case is not a 'hard case.' Here FitzPatrick assumes a wholly implausible picture of how moral learning occurs. Many people have false moral beliefs although they have thought carefully about the questions at issue and they have not violated any procedural norms. For example, for many business practices that are in fact reprehensibly ruthless, we can find plenty of businesspeople ready to offer elaborate, sustained, and serious moral defenses of them. We can also find people who have entered the business world, heard arguments on all sides, and become convinced of the wrong view of business morality.

FitzPatrick wants to preserve many of our claims of ordinary blameworthiness. He wants to vindicate the claim that immoral business practices, which we ordinarily take to be blameworthy, are blameworthy; and he wants to vindicate the claim that the actions of the Bush Administration regarding Afghanistan and Iraq are blameworthy. FitzPatrick quotes those who have commented that George W. Bush himself was remarkably incurious; it does appear that Bush is guilty of mismanagement of his beliefs. But presumably FitzPatrick thinks that all the important players in the Bush administration are blameworthy, and it is far from clear that they all are guilty of mismanagement of their beliefs. Some of them appear to have had a well-thought-out, though extreme, agenda.[13]

It's important that moral knowledge isn't *easy* to come by, and isn't assured if one manages one's beliefs well, not even if one is exposed to good moral arguments for the truth.

My point is this:

> Someone may have been perfectly responsible regarding procedural norms for the management of his beliefs while nevertheless having come to deeply false moral views, even where he is perfectly aware of substantial disagreement. This is true regarding most interesting moral claims, including claims about how businesspeople should behave, how people in government should behave, how we should treat our children, etc. It is true of most (if not all) ordinary moral claims.

FitzPatrick supposes that it is only in 'hard cases' that someone may think seriously about morality, in the face of views that oppose his own, and come to the wrong view. And he claims that business ethics and the ethics of government are not hard cases. Unfortunately, ethics is not that easy: if we use 'hard cases' in FitzPatrick's sense, then most cases are hard cases.

I will draw three lessons from my discussion of these four objections to Rosen. First, it is not at all plausible that mere ignorance exculpates; at best, it is false belief that exculpates. Second, motivated ignorance may be blameworthy although it is not the result of an earlier instance of clear-eyed *akrasia*. Third, some mismanagement of belief may be blameworthy without involving clear-eyed *akrasia*. Taking these lessons into account, it may seem that Rosen's argument still supports the following:

Narrower Conclusion:

If

(a) a person acts wrongly while believing a false claim, p,

(b) if p is true then the action is permissible,

(c) the false belief did not result from mismanagement of belief, and

---

[13] We should not be misled by the fact that they were incurious about some things, such as the truth about global warming: there were some things they wanted little information about because they were determined to act in a particular way regardless of that information.

(d) the false belief is not a case of motivated ignorance, then

the person is blameless for so acting.

Clauses (a) and (b) place a restriction to cases of false beliefs that license the action, taking the first objection seriously. Clause (c) restricts us to cases that do not involve mismanagement of beliefs. Note that this restriction is more restrictive than is necessary in light of the fourth objection. I am restricting in this way to set the fourth objection aside. Clause (d) restricts us to cases that do not involve motivated ignorance, taking the third objection seriously.

3. The Significance of the Narrower Conclusion

The Narrower Conclusion is still quite strong; it implies that in many ordinary cases of apparent blameworthiness, the agents are in fact blameless. I will now describe a number of cases in which we would ordinarily take the agents to be blameworthy, but the Narrower Conclusion implies they are not. I stipulate for all of these cases that clauses (c) and (d) apply. It is important to emphasize this stipulation because it is easy to imagine variants of the cases in which either motivated ignorance or mismanagement of beliefs does play a role. Nevertheless, there are many actual cases of the types I will outline in which ordinary people come to false moral views without having mismanaged their beliefs. In many of the cases below, I stipulate that the agents have thought long and seriously about the relevant moral questions, have considered opposing views, and have come to false moral views. In some of the cases, the agents are not aware that people might disagree with them; these agents have not thought particularly hard about the moral views in question, but they have thought an ordinary amount about morality in general, and so they have not violated any procedural norms.

As I've already suggested, one case is that of a businessman who has thought seriously about the ethics of business and who has concluded that what are in fact 'reprehensibly ruthless' practices are really 'permissibly aggressive.' This businessman is bothered by the fact that some people criticize his practices. He isn't surprised that those who are hurt by the practices say they are ruthless, but it bothers him that his brother says so. He discusses it at length with his brother and also with others. He comes to the view that it is better for the economy overall if companies operate to maximize profits, and that economic progress always has casualties. He believes that by pursuing what is in the best interests of his shareholders, he is playing a valuable role in the economy. This is not a great view. But someone may well have thought seriously about the morality of business practices and come to such a view. Indeed, many actual businesspeople have thought about the morality of business, have not been irresponsible in the management of their opinions, and have false views that license their behavior.

Two more examples are variants of cases Rosen discusses. One is a case of a 1950s American father who doesn't save to send his daughter to college but does save to send his sons to college: he is a sexist in his treatment of his children. The other is an ancient Hittite slaveholder who keeps slaves. Rosen stipulates that these two agents do not believe their actions are wrong. He says they do not think about whether the actions are wrong at all. In the versions of the cases I will focus on, the agents have *implicit* moral beliefs that their actions are permissible. (It's not clear if this is what Rosen has in mind.[14]) I stipulate that these agents care about being moral and they think about morality to a reasonable degree.

Another kind of case involves people who are raised to believe in an ethics of 'everyone should take care of his own.' Consider three cases along these lines. One is someone raised in a Mafia family who goes into the family business and believes in an ethics of deep loyalty to the family business group and no moral obligations to those beyond it; this man kills a store owner who won't 'pay for protection'. Another is someone raised in a tribal group that is in conflict with other nearby tribal groups; he kills a member of a rival group in order to assert his own group's dominance. Finally, consider someone raised in a poor neighborhood of an American inner city. He joins a gang and believes that one should show deep loyalty to one's own and one should be willing to do anything to

---

[14]   Guerrero 'Don't Know, Don't Kill' discusses several variants of Rosen's cases, in some of which the agents simply *lack beliefs* about whether their actions are wrong, rather than having beliefs that their actions are permissible. As Guerrero points out – this is an instance of the first objection I discussed – mere lack of belief that one's action is wrong does not exculpate.

others for the sake of the gang. These three agents have not been irresponsible in the management of their beliefs. Let's suppose that the tribe member is not aware of other moral views. The Mafia member and the gang member are aware of people who disagree with the moral views they hold. But they believe others have been suckered into a false sense of their duties.

Another kind of case is given by actions which are currently deeply morally contested; I will give three such examples. In giving these examples, I make controversial moral claims; but these claims are not crucial to my points in this paper. Consider someone who believes abortion is wrong and who yells at women outside abortion clinics. It is wrong to yell at women outside abortion clinics: these women are already having a hard time and making their difficult decision more psychologically painful is wrong. But this person acts in a way that would be permissible if her moral views were true. Another example is someone who believes abortion is wrong and who kills an abortion doctor, in a part of the country where there is good reason to think that this doctor's death will reduce the number of abortions. This person believes that he ought to kill abortion doctors if doing so would reduce the number of abortions that would be performed. A third example is someone who believes homosexuality is wrong who organizes a campaign against the legalization of gay marriage. He believes he is doing something morally good in organizing the campaign; in fact, in working to further oppression, he is acting wrongly.[15]

I have stipulated that in all of the above cases, the agents have not violated any procedural norms to do with the management of their beliefs. Someone might object that some of the moral views in these cases are *too crazy* for anyone to have come to them without having behaved poorly in the management of her beliefs. But that seems manifestly false.

These examples show that, if the Narrower Conclusion is true, then in many cases in which we would ordinarily take people to be blameworthy, they are in fact blameless. The Narrower Conclusion is thus significant and deeply implausible.

---

[15] If my controversial claims are false, then different examples should be used to make my point. For example, if abortion is morally wrong, then a doctor who believes abortion is permissible is nevertheless blameworthy for performing abortions.

4. My Proposed View

I will now propose a view on which the actions I have just described are indeed blameworthy, as they appear to be. The view I propose denies Rosen's claim that actions done by agents with false moral beliefs cannot be loci of original responsibility. However, the view grants that there is something right about Rosen's position. In particular, it cannot be that a person is blameworthy for a wrong action he believed to be permissible but is blameless for his false belief. While denying that the blameworthiness for the wrong action *is derivative* from the blameworthiness for the belief, the view holds that in such cases the action is blameworthy *only if* the belief is blameworthy as well.

On the view I propose, one can be blameworthy for having false moral beliefs although one has not been in any way irresponsible in the management of one's opinion: one may not have acted in any way procedurally badly. Rather, one has violated some moral norms that apply to *beliefs* themselves, not to the management of one's beliefs. The view holds that we morally ought to believe the moral truth.

Here is the proposed view:

> We are morally obligated to believe the moral truths relevant to our actions (and thus not to believe false moral claims relevant to our actions), and we are often blameworthy for failing to meet these moral obligations, even if we have not been guilty of mismanagement of our beliefs, and even if our ignorance is not motivated.

> Wrong actions that result from false moral beliefs are not thereby blameless; indeed, they may be loci of *original* responsibility. While both the beliefs and the actions are blameworthy, the actions are not blameworthy *because* the beliefs are blameworthy. Rather, the actions and the beliefs are blameworthy for similar reasons.

These are the essential components of the view. I propose the view to show what an alternative picture to Rosen's could look like, while capturing some of what is plausible about his view (namely, that if the actions in these cases are blameworthy, then the beliefs are too) without resulting in his implausible conclusions.

So far the view leaves open what ultimately explains blameworthiness. One way of spelling out the view further would be to appeal to Nomy Arpaly's view of blameworthiness:[16]

> An action is blameworthy just in case the action resulted from the agent's caring inadequately about what is morally significant – where this is not a matter of *de dicto* caring about morality but *de re* caring about what is in fact morally significant.

(One *de dicto* cares about morality if one desires *to act morally*. One *de re* cares about what is in fact morally significant if, for example, one desires *not to cause others' suffering* (and this is in fact morally significant).[17])

We might furthermore expand the view beyond Arpaly's own development of it:[18]

> Beliefs (and failures to believe) are blameworthy if they involve inadequately caring about what is morally significant. Believing a certain kind of behavior is wrong on the basis of a certain consideration is a way of caring about that consideration.

> Some failures to believe moral truths relevant to one's actions are not blameworthy. For example, if one blamelessly falsely believes a non-moral claim, and this leads to one's false moral belief, then one's false moral belief does not involve inadequately caring about what is morally significant.

5. Objections to the Proposed View

I will now discuss some objections to the proposed view. This discussion will bring out some further aspects of the view.

The first objection:

> In the cases described in section 3, the agents who act wrongly have *epistemically justified* false moral beliefs that their actions

---

[16] Nomy Arpaly, *Unprincipled Virtue* (Oxford: Oxford University Press, 2003).

[17] Exactly what is involved in *de re* caring about morality depends on the true moral view. On some views, promise-breaking is morally significant; on these views, desiring *not to break promises* would be an instance of caring about what is in fact morally significant. But if utilitarianism is true, then promise-breaking is not morally significant, and this desire would not be an instance of caring about what is in fact morally significant.

[18] I believe this is an expansion of Arpaly's view, but perhaps she intended this to be part of her view.

are permissible. Surely they cannot be blameworthy for having beliefs that are epistemically justified (since they haven't mismanaged their beliefs). But then they cannot be blameworthy for acting *on* their reasonable beliefs.

In favor of the claim that the agents' beliefs are epistemically justified, the objector might offer the following considerations. First, some of the agents' evidence is *testimonial*: people they reasonably take to be authorities about morality have made the claims they believe. Second, many of them have considered arguments for and against their views and they have been convinced by seemingly compelling arguments. Third, some of the considerations they rely on to support their views do genuinely *tell in favor of* their beliefs. Fourth, they have genuinely tried hard to think about the issue and upon reflection have arrived at their views. When we focus on the way that they came to their beliefs and their judgments that their beliefs are the right response to their evidence, it may appear that their beliefs are justified. (This applies to those agents who've considered the moral issue carefully, not to those who haven't considered it at all, such as the slaveholder.)

My response to the objection is that the agents' beliefs are not epistemically justified. Consideration of fallacious, though seductive, lines of thought is not a way of coming to have justified beliefs. Someone who is suckered in by a sneaky instance of affirming the consequent is not justified merely by its having seemed to him that the considerations he relies on do support the conclusion he draws. While testimony can lead to justified belief, we have stipulated that in many of these cases the agents are not *merely* relying on testimony. Consideration of evidence which shows a claim to be false can undermine testimonial justification for the claim.

The objector's claim that the agents' false moral beliefs are epistemically justified is more compelling regarding those agents who are not aware that there is disagreement about their ethical beliefs; these agents hold these beliefs on the basis of testimony, and have not thought the moral questions through for themselves. Nevertheless, this does not show that their beliefs are epistemically justified. It is a hard question what constitutes evidence for moral claims, and in what circumstances a person's evidence is such that the right response to the evidence – the epistemically responsible response – involves believing the moral truth about a certain matter. But I claim that ordinary people who know the non-moral facts of what they are doing, when they do wrong things, often do have *sufficient evidence* that their actions are wrong. For this reason, their beliefs that their actions are permissible are unjustified. (This is a substantive and controversial claim I will not defend here.)

My considered view is that the agents in all of the cases I described in section 3 do not have epistemically justified beliefs. But if they do have epistemically justified beliefs, I accept the implication of my proposed view that they are blameworthy for having beliefs that are epistemically justified, and they are blameworthy for acting on those beliefs.[19] I see their cases as instances of constitutive moral bad luck: they are unlucky to have found themselves in circumstances that have caused them to be (in some respects) morally bad people.

The second objection to the proposed view:

> The beliefs in question are epistemically justified, so believing otherwise would be epistemically unjustified. We cannot be morally required to believe in a way that would be epistemically unjustified.

Like the first objection, this objection claims that the beliefs in question are epistemically justified. I will grant for the sake of argument the second objection's claim that the agents' beliefs are epistemically justified.

My response is that there can be cases in which a person is epistemically justified in believing p, but p is false, and she is *in a position to realize* that p is false, such that she would become epistemically justified in believing not-p: she is in a position to become justified in believing not-p. For example, consider the following case. I studied some advanced math in college, but that was years ago. My friend Moon, who has a PhD in math, might tell me that a particular mathematical claim, p, is true. I may

---

[19]   There is independent reason to think that people can be blameworthy for having epistemically justified beliefs, and for acting on these beliefs (even when the blameworthiness cannot be traced to earlier wrong behavior). Simon Keller ('Friendship and Belief,' *Philosophical Papers* 33 (2004), 329–351) and Sarah Stroud ('Epistemic Partiality in Friendship' *Ethics* 116 (2006), 498–524) have argued that we owe our friends the benefit of the doubt, such that we ought to refrain from believing ill of them in some cases in which such beliefs would be epistemically justified. On this view, someone who thinks ill of a friend when she owes it to her friend to withhold belief is blameworthy for her belief; and if she acts wrongly on the basis of the belief, it seems she is blameworthy for so acting.

remember enough math to fully understand what p says. I come to believe p on the basis of Moon's testimony, and I am justified in so believing. However, p is false, and I still remember enough of the relevant math that I *could* realize p is false and I could come up with a proof of not-p. It is not assured that if I try to think about whether p is true, I will have this realization; it may not come to me. But I could have this realization; I am *capable* of having it. Thus, while my belief in p is epistemically justified, I am in a position to become justified in believing not-p: I have the mathematical tools to go through a thought process that would undermine my justification for believing p and render me justified in believing not-p. This case is analogous to the case of people who have false moral beliefs (if, as I am granting to the objector, those beliefs are epistemically justified): they *could* realize the moral truth, though for many of them there may be no guarantee that they will if they try.

The third objection:

> One can't be blameworthy for something's not *occurring* to one, even if it's *possible* that it occur to one, and particularly if there's no particular step one might have taken that would have ensured that it occur to one.

This objection is a natural response to what I have said in response to the second and third objections. However, the claim the objector makes is simply false. One can be blameworthy for something's not occurring to one. A parent who forgets to pick her child up at school is blameworthy for forgetting, even in a case in which she took what everyone would agree are reasonable precautions against forgetting. A doctor who forgets to check a chart for an allergy is blameworthy for forgetting, even in a case in which she took what everyone would agree are reasonable precautions about forgetting. Of course *forgetting* is different from *failing to realize*, though both are cases of something's not occurring to one. The objector might grant that one can be blameworthy for *forgetting* while denying that one can be blameworthy for not *realizing* something. But there are counterexamples to that claim too. Suppose that we simultaneously experience a blackout and smell a gas leak, and I decide to light a match to navigate my way through the building. I do not *realize* that this may cause an explosion. I *could* realize it, but there's no particular step I could have taken that would have ensured that I realize it. I may still be blameworthy for my failure to realize, and for risking an explosion. By its nature, *realizing* something, like *remembering* something, is such that when one is capable of doing it, it's also true that one might fail to do it; and is such that there is no particular step one can take to ensure that one do it, short of already doing it.

6. Understanding My Disagreement with Rosen

In this section, I will step back and make some general comments aimed at illuminating the dispute over whether this claim, to which Rosen is committed, is true:

Weaker Lesson:
If an agent acts wrongly while falsely believing that p, and if p were true then her action would be morally permissible, *then* the agent's action is not a locus of original responsibility: if she is blameworthy for acting, then she is so blameworthy only in virtue of being blameworthy for her false belief.

My proposed view is just one instance of a family of possible views on which Weaker Lesson is false. In this section, I will set aside the further features of my proposed view and focus on my dispute with Rosen regarding Weaker Lesson.

Weaker Lesson is supposed to be supported by the case of Anne, who spoons cyanide into Bill's coffee while thinking it is sugar (and who is blameless for her false belief). Anne is blameless for poisoning Bill; Rosen would say that Weaker Lesson tells the right story about why she is blameless. Anne's belief that she is spooning sugar is such that, if it were true, her action would be permissible, and she is blameless for having this belief. These two facts, according to Rosen, are why she is blameless.

I think Anne's blamelessness stems not from the *presence* of a particular false belief, but from the *absence* of any beliefs that make her blameworthy. I think the right lesson to draw is this:

The Right Lesson:
If an agent acts wrongly and nothing in her epistemic state can ground her blameworthiness for acting as she does, *then* the agent's action is not a locus of original responsibility: if she is blameworthy for so acting, then she is so blameworthy only in virtue of being blameworthy for her epistemic state.

There is nothing at all in Anne's epistemic state to which we could appeal to ground her blameworthiness. She does not knowingly do something morally wrong; nor does she knowingly poison someone; nor does she knowingly risk poisoning someone, etc.[20]

Rosen should agree with me that the Right Lesson makes a true claim. My disagreement with Rosen is not over whether the Right Lesson is true, but over what in an agent's epistemic state can ground her blameworthiness for acting as she does. Rosen thinks that an agent who knowingly enslaves another, who does not know that doing so is wrong, *lacks* anything in his epistemic state which grounds blameworthiness for his action. I disagree. I think that knowingly enslaving someone is itself blameworthy: the feature of the slaveholder's epistemic state that renders him blameworthy is his knowledge that he is enslaving someone. (While Rosen should agree with me that Right Lesson is true, he will hold that Weaker Lesson (or a claim along its lines) is also true and is explained by Right Lesson; I deny this.)

I am now in a position to tie up a loose end from my earlier discussion.

In section 2, I discussed the example of a doctor who forgets to check the chart to see whether her patient is allergic to the drug she is going to administer; I said the doctor, who does not think of whether to check the chart, has no false belief such that if it were true her action would be permissible. On the contrary, she knows that she is administering a drug, she knows that she is not currently checking the chart, and she knows that in such cases she ought to check the chart; she is not explicitly thinking about these facts, but she does know all of them. In footnote 9 I mentioned the objection that the doctor must have an implicit belief that she is not currently doing anything wrong. My response to this objection is that *even if* the doctor has that implicit belief, that is not enough to show that her action is not a source of original responsibility: while she may have that implicit belief, her *whole epistemic state*

---

[20] Note that the Right Lesson is compatible with a view on which it is a *global* question whether an agent's epistemic state renders her action blameworthy: some beliefs may ground blameworthiness for Aing in one case, but the same beliefs would not ground blameworthiness for Aing if other beliefs are present. (For example, Sam may be blameworthy for knowingly pushing someone to the ground. But Bob may not be blameworthy though he knowingly pushed someone to the ground, since Bob had the further belief that this was the only way to save that person's life.)

Indeed my objection to Weaker Lesson is that it does not allow the *whole* of a person's epistemic state to determine whether she is blameworthy.

includes knowledge of facts that render her action blameworthy. When deciding whether a person's epistemic state gets her off the hook – such that if she is blameworthy at all, it is only for being in that epistemic state – we must consider the *whole* of her epistemic state, not merely a single belief within it.

(The example of the doctor who forgets to check the chart highlights a more general phenomenon: that a person holds a particular belief such that, if true, her action would be permissible, does not ensure that she does not hold other beliefs which straightforwardly imply her action is impermissible. Rosen thinks that whether a person is blameworthy crucially depends on the person's moral beliefs. But given cases in which a person's moral beliefs are not fully coherent, even he should deny Weaker Lesson. I am not sure how to state the best version of his view.[21])

The dispute between Rosen and me regarding Weaker Lesson (suitably fixed up) should be understood as a dispute about whether the Right Lesson implies Weaker Lesson. Rosen and I agree that Anne's blamelessness is explained by her epistemic state; but we disagree about what features of her epistemic state make her blameless, and what the lesson is for cases of moral false belief. We also disagree about how much *help* consideration of Anne's case gives us when we turn to consider cases of agents who act wrongly, with full factual information but with false moral beliefs. I think all we learn from Anne's case is that a person's epistemic situation, considered as a whole, may contain no features which ground her blameworthiness, even though she is acting wrongly.

My claim that Anne's case (or any case of mere non-moral ignorance) does not provide the lesson Rosen draws is further bolstered by reflection on the stated version of Rosen's view, which is that Anne's *ignorance* renders her blameless. Rosen does

---

[21]   One possible revision of the lesson is the following, which Rosen has suggested to me in conversation about cases of uncertainty: an agent who is ignorant that her action is wrong *in any sense* (either objectively wrong or subjectively wrong) is blameworthy for acting only if (and only because) she is blameworthy for her ignorance. With this revision, Rosen can acknowledge that Alice is blameworthy when she spoons what she has a .5 credence is cyanide into Bob's coffee: Alice knows that taking a 50% risk of poisoning someone is wrong. But this revision will not correctly handle cases that involve uncertainty whether an action is subjectively wrong: an agent who acts wrongly with 50% credence her action is subjectively wrong is blameworthy for so acting (if she knows the alternative is subjectively permissible). More seriously, this revision runs into the problem I lay out in the final paragraph of this section.

not characterize the ignorance Anne has, and so when he says that his principles regarding ignorance apply *in full generality* (that is, to moral ignorance as well as factual ignorance), he faces a problem. The relevant principle is that an agent who acts in ignorance is blameworthy for acting only if (and only because) she is blameworthy for her ignorance. This principle is elliptical; not any ignorance will do, so we must characterize the ignorance. Rosen's principle could be read as either of the following claims. (a) An agent who acts wrongly in ignorance of every fact that is sufficient for the wrongness of her action is blameworthy for acting only if (and only because) she is blameworthy for this ignorance.[22,23] Or (b) an agent who acts wrongly in ignorance *that* her action is wrong is blameworthy for acting only if (and only because) she is blameworthy for this ignorance. The problem Rosen faces is that he needs to be appealing to principle (b); principle (a) does not have the implications he draws for cases of moral ignorance.[24] However, the case of Anne does not support (b); while Anne's case supports (a), reflection on Anne's case need not lead anyone to endorse (b). Whether (b) is plausible depends on whether one thinks moral ignorance is exculpating; (b) gains no independent plausibility from consideration of Anne's blamelessness.

7. Conclusion

I have discussed some objections to Rosen's Broad Conclusion and argued that, even in the face of these objections, Rosen's arguments still may appear to support the Narrower Conclusion, which has sweeping and implausible implications. I have described some cases of actions which are blameworthy but which the Narrower Conclusion implies are blameless. I have proposed a view on which these actions are blameworthy, contrary to Rosen's view. I have defended the view against some objections. I have not independently argued for the proposed view, though it is

---

[22] I state the principle in this way to cover cases in which an action is wrong for two independent reasons; an agent ignorant of the fact that makes his action wrong in one way is not blameless if he is aware of the other fact that makes his action wrong.

[23] Note that each fact sufficient for the wrongness of an action will be a complex fact.

[24] An agent who is morally ignorant but not factually ignorant knows her factual situation, and so knows a fact sufficient for the wrongness of her action.

supported by the claim that the actions I described are indeed blameworthy. I have not aimed to establish the proposed view, but to set it out as an alternative to the picture Rosen offers. Finally, I have argued that consideration of cases in which false non-moral beliefs exculpate does not support Rosen's view that false moral beliefs exculpate.

INDEX

References are to page numbers and their footnotes indicated by 'n', e.g. 35n.

Developing Deontology, First Edition. Edited by Brad Hooker. Copyright © 2012 The Authors. Book
compilation © 2012 Blackwell Publishing Ltd.